Win-Win Partnerships

Be On The Leading Edge With Synergistic Coaching

Steven J. Stowell, Ph.D.   Matt M. Starcevich, Ph.D.

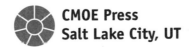

CMOE Press
Salt Lake City, UT

CMOE, Inc.
9146 South 700 East
Sandy, UT 84070

Library of Congress Cataloging-in-Publication Data
Stowell, Steven J. and Starcevich, Matthew M.
Win-Win Partnerships—Be On The Leading Edge With
Synergistic Coaching

Includes bibliographical references
ISBN-10: 0-9724627-1-6
ISBN-13: 978-0-9724627-1-6

First Edition
Fourteenth Printing, May 2016

Editing: Helen Hodgson & Brent Yorgason
Copyediting & Word Processing: Debbie Stowell & Stephanie Stowell
Cover Design: Randy Smith & Associates
Graphic Design/Desktop Publishing: In Plain English, Inc.

Ordering Information

Orders by individuals and organizations. This book and other publications are available by ordering direct from the publisher at the CMOE Press at (801) 569-3444 or www.cmoe.com. Discounts on bulk quantities are available.

CMOE Press
9146 South 700 East
Sandy, Utah 84070

Suggested Reading

Also by Steven J. Stowell, Ph.D. &
Matt M. Starcevich, Ph.D.

The Coach—Creating Partnerships For A
Competitive Edge

Teamwork—We Have Met The Enemy and
They Are Us

Acknowledgements

We dedicate this book to the 100,000 men and women in our client organizations who in turn dedicate themselves to coaching and learning. We know it isn't easy standing strong in the face of pressure and frustrations of life.

Abbott Labs
Alberto Enviro Fuels
Allyska Pipeline
Amdahl
American Cancer Society
American Dental Association
American Express
American Investment Bank
Ameritech
Armstrong World Industries
ATF
AT&T
Avis Rent-A-Car
Baker Oil Tool
Bank of Montreal
BDM
Becton Dickinson
Bell Canada
BellSouth
BF Goodrich
Blue Cross Blue Shield
Boeing
Boy Scouts of America
Canadian Space Agency
Canned Foods
Cargill
Carter Mining
Chevron Chemical
ChevronTexaco
Chic-Fil-A
Church's Chicken
CIBA Corning
ConocoPhillips
Control Concepts
Countrywide
Covance Laboratories
Credit Union Executive Society
Cutco
Delphi
Delta Airlines

Department of Energy
DHL Global
Dow Brands
Dun & Bradstreet
Duracell
EDS
EG&G
Elf Autochem
Enviro Tech
Executive Women International
EXXON
FAA
Family Life
Fannie Mae
FBI
FedEx
Florence Bus Company
Florida Power
FMC
Formosa Plastics
Freddie Mac
Furon Company
GE Appliances
GE Capital
GE Computer
General Chemical
GM/Volvo Heavy Trucks
Granite Construction
Grifols, Inc.
Halliburton
Harris Bank
Hastings Manufacturing
Hennessy Industries
Hershey Foods
Hertz
HP
Home Savings of America
Honeywell
Independence Mining
J.M. Huber

Johnson Controls
Johnsonville Foods
Jones Intercable
Kaiser Permanente
Kennecott Corporation
Knauf Insulation
Koch Industries
L3
Lang Drilling
LDS Business College
Lemington Coal
Lennox
Lockheed Martin
Los Alamos National Labs
M & T Bank
Mass Mutual
Matador Cattle Company
Maxus Energy
McCormick
McDonnell Douglas
Meijer, Inc.
Meloche Mennox
Merridian Minerals
Michigan Wheel
Miles, Inc.
Minera Alumberera
Minnesota Power
Minnesota State Patrol
Mitre Corporation
Mobil Oil
Monsanto
Monterey Coal
Motorola
Motovario
Navy Underwater Warfare Center
Nielsen Media
Newmont
Novacore
NYPD
Occidental USA
Oliver Products
Organon
Orlando Sentinel
P&M Cedar Products
Pacific Gas & Electric
Paradies Shops
PepsiCo
Perdue Frederick
Pfizer
Philadelphia Electric

Pioneer Hi-Bred
Printpack
Qwest
Ralston Foods
Research Cottrell
R.J. Reynolds
Rohm & Haas
Rosewood Medical Center
7-Eleven
Sandia National Lab
Sargent & Lundy
Sauer-Danfoss
Schlegel
Sears Canada
Segment Computer
Sequent Computers
Siemens
Smith's Foods
Social Security Administration
Soges - Italy
Southwestern Bell
Southern Company
Southern New England Telephone
State of Idaho
Steelcase
Stentor
Superior Bank
Sylvania
Teledyne Water Pik
Tesoro
Trinity Industries
Tulsa County
Turner Broadcasting
UAW/Ford
Ulan Coal
Union Electric
Unisys
Upjohn Canada
U.S. Air Force
US Bank
U.S. Postal Service
U.S. Steel
USX Corporation
Utah Highway Patrol
Utah Transit Authority
Vistakon, Inc.
Weight Watchers
Wells Fargo Financial
Weston Bakeries
Whittier Oil

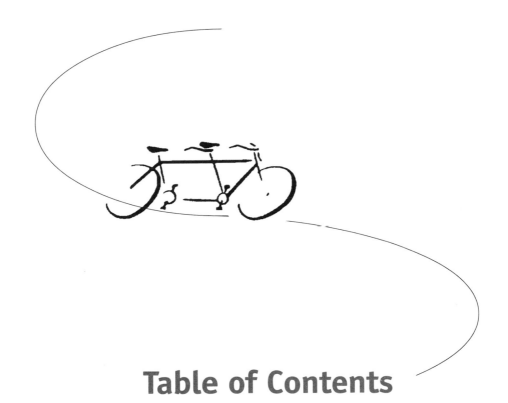

Table of Contents

Table of Contents

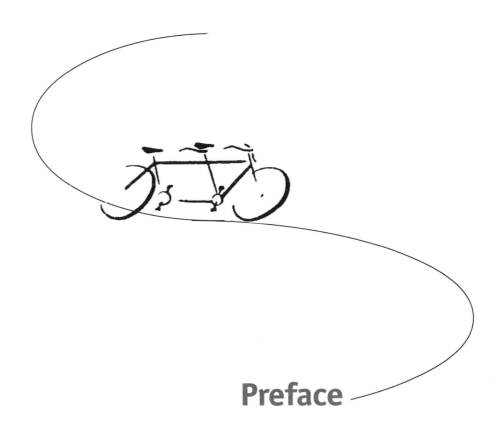

Preface

Preface

It is difficult to accomplish anything of real value in this life unless you have positive interaction and relationships.

In 1987, when we published our book, *THE COACH: Creating Partnerships For A Competitive Edge,* we did so with a decade of experience under our belts. We intuitively felt coaching was good for people who care about their relationships, want to grow, and contribute. The decade since then has been a fascinating journey—a journey that has taken us to interesting places and people in our search for answers and inquiry into the meaning of coaching.

We decided to write more about coaching and partnerships partly because the people we serve have asked for additional help in developing the skills we see in successful relationships. However, our chief reason is that we really enjoy seeing the synergistic teamwork between people blossom. We see the positive changes and improvements in our own organization, and in individual lives, when we strive to be good coaching partners. In short, we are riveted to coaching because of the fulfillment we receive.

Coaching has elevated and enhanced the quality of our communications and the richness in our lives.

In our writing, we are not trying to display creative genius. Some suggestions are not radically new. In some cases, we amplify on, and broaden, a few concepts outlined in our original book. Our fundamental assertion is that coaching is a very practical way to function with others who join with us to achieve common objectives and goals.

What is coaching **?** and how does it work in organizations?

When we began our original study of coaching 20 years ago, it seemed that, outside of sports and marriage, little was known about coaching or partnerships. Whenever we spoke or presented our seminar, we were asked: "What is coaching?" "How does it work in organizations?" "Can coaching also be used within the framework of the family, the school, and the community?" "Just when *can* it best be used, and who *should* use it?" "Is there a payback?" These questions caused us to consider whether we had underestimated the interest and wide application of this exciting process. Something is definitely evolving that is causing people in all facets of life to stop, bend an ear, and seek to understand how to build partnerships that work.

Coordinated Effort

We concluded our last book on coaching with this thought: "A person can only achieve their potential greatness through relationships with others." This is still our core belief today. Think about it for a minute. Nearly everything we achieve is ultimately the result of a combined effort or partnership with others. Sometimes, those who are assisting may be in a very passive role, like a good audience that appreciates the performance of a fine symphony. Or the partnership may be more direct, like the technical assistance a trainer gives an Olympic athlete, or the exchange that occurs between a doctor and a patient in a highly successful medical intervention.

A person can only achieve their potential greatness through relationships with others.

Partnerships are commonplace in business, in our families, and in recreational activities.

Nearly every-
thing we do can
be done better
if we team up
with a coach.

The media highlights the dynamics of combined
efforts in the performance of famous athletes like
Jerry Rice and Steve Young of the San Francisco 49ers.
It is also apparent when you watch the all-time
professional assist leader, John Stockton, set up his
teammate, Karl Malone, and the result is that they
jointly achieve high assist and high point totals year
after year. Each of these performances hinges on.
coordinated effort. While it is true that any one of
these individuals is an amazing performer in his own
right, when you combine two good talents into an
effective partnership, magic and synergy begin to
unfold. When a relationship clicks, and then becomes
cemented, it is hard to defeat.

That is the phenomenon that we address in this book.
How do you coordinate? How do you build these
strategic alliances and networks? How can you offer

A Skating Partnership

The principle of a win-win partnership was
beautifully illustrated by the artistic skating of
Ekaterina Gordeeva and Sergei Grinkov.
When his heart stopped during practice in late
1995, it was tragic and shocking to all of us
who enjoyed watching this storybook partnership develop. First
in Russia, then in a gold medal partnership in Calgary in 1988,
and again in Lillehammer in 1994. Good partnerships transcend
cultural and economic idealogies. It wasn't always perfect for
Gordeeva and Grinkov. No one could foresee the power in this
pair when they were first teamed by their Soviet coaches in 1982.
She was a skinny 11 year old and he was 15. But six years later the
partnership bloomed into gold. They were committed to the task,
they coached each other and they listened to the input of others in
the skating community. It wasn't quite the same when she skated
solo for the first time in 1996 after his death. There is just something magical about a partnership that catches our imagination.

help to others? How do you open the door of communication?

Sometimes it is not easy to address opportunities, needs, or problems without creating a backlash of resentment, frustration, or resistance from others. We all need to develop our talent to effectively and less aggressively disclose our perceptions, as well as to accept and discuss the "blind spots" in our own efforts. We need to learn to be open and flexible, as well as skillful, at giving and receiving assistance. So much of our lives—our education system, the business world, sports—is spent learning how to be competitive. So much of the world is focused on building individual thinking skills, self-reliance, and self-confidence.

Society needs more partnerships; we don't need more rogue individuals and mavericks.

Don't get us wrong. We are not suggesting that a sense of competitiveness and self-reliance are "bad" things. Carried to an extreme in the wrong situation, competitiveness can harm key alliances, partnerships, and coalitions that are so critical to our overall, long-term success. The leader who is in conflict with a team member can cause losses in productivity and satisfaction for both people. When a teacher and student can't agree on proper classroom behavior, it can negatively impact the entire class. Parents and children who cannot reach an understanding about taking the responsibility for an automobile or a pet, or members of a charity organizer who cannot create a common strategy for raising funds, jeopardize the success of their relationship and service.

Competition is like blood pressure. Too much or too little can be disastrous to our well-being.

Very simply, the job of a coach is to discover the needs and will of the partners, and to then discover the needs and requirements of the organization. The coach then blends and creates synergy through superior "world class communication." Partners who

Effective partnering is about recognizing talent, developing it, and then blending the talents of diverse individuals.

coach are easy to talk to, and they create learning moments. In a broad sense, effective partnering is about recognizing talent, developing it, and then blending the talents of diverse individuals. The objective is to weave the knowledge, skills, and ideas of individuals to achieve creative solutions.

The focus of this book is on creating positive conditions for discovering and acting on growth opportunities.

The essence of coaching centers on building interactions that are safe and that enable the other parties to offer up their ideas and to share information, thoughts, and feelings. Coaching involves skills that lower defense mechanisms so that others can accept input, suggestions, and direction.

In the final analysis, effective coaching creates true collaboration and synergy. It focuses on coordinated effort and how we create a unique chemistry that brings excitement to our relationships, as well as productive results to our organizations. To make this happen, coaching partners need to use good judgment and skills so that they can support, confront, and listen to each other.

Strong relationships are the core of high-performance teams.

Joint Ventures—Many people "sign on" with organizations to contribute to a *joint venture*. They want to grow, fulfill their potential, find satisfaction, and make a contribution to the group's mission.

Synergistic coaching is an important skill, primarily because when done successfully, it enhances communication. Good interaction and dialogue are common phenomena of successful organizations from ancient times. Communication is the core of every good team that we have assisted over the past

20 years. The coaching style of communication helps people feel connected to each other and creates a sense of belonging. When people don't interact successfully, a void exists and people don't feel in partnership in their endeavors with each other. **Coaching interactions, on the other hand, lead to a pool of shared knowledge, experience, judgment, and perception.** As people talk and exchange views, the partnership becomes very potent.

Coaching is more than artfully putting words together. Coaching aims to connect people in genuinely meaningful ways and with deeper understanding to spark thoughts and ideas. It generates positive, long-term feelings of mutual respect and interest. It also creates mental images and pictures of success. The goal of coaching is to engage all the senses as efforts are aligned and synchronized. Synergistic coaching is not the "end all." It doesn't always work miracles. Because coaching is a two-party system, its success depends on willingness and openness from both partners to be less partisan.

Coaching is a two-party system; its success depends on willingness and openness from both partners to be less partisan.

It's Not A Perfect World

We are not asking you to be a perfect partner or coach. As much as we have studied the coaching phenomenon, we are still learning, and are far from perfection ourselves. We are all "coaching challenged" to some degree. Still, we keep working at it. While coaching isn't always the perfect answer, it is always worth a try. It is a place to start when working through decisions, problems, and exciting but risky new opportunities.

In this book, you will discover an amalgam of ideas, skills, guidelines, and principles that will be of value when you choose to be in the coaching role. It will help you with the requirements and mileposts that must be addressed as you venture into new territory. Coaching certainly requires some dedication and vigor. It is a deliberate process, not a casual activity. **You must rigorously commit to "walking the talk."** It isn't enough to conceptually learn this material. Practice and direct experience are essential to improve your contribution to a partnership. It is truly more natural and human to be controlling, autocratic, and self-focused than to be committed to building unanimity, consensus, and synergy. It is easy to get lost and to ignore the signs that this has happened.

When you coach, information flows, minds open up to different ideas, and learning occurs.

If you are willing to concentrate on the messages, and to really try them out, you can reap the rewards of greater loyalty, commitment, and innovation from your partners. When you coach, you protect and build the emotional investment that others have in the association. You will see information flow, minds open up to different ideas, and learning occur.

We must coach whenever we have the opportunity, because, unfortunately, we sometimes "mess up." We do things that we don't intend on doing. Sometimes we even do things we have previously determined not to do. These actions create setbacks with our partners that coaching can help reverse.

Self-Coaching

Coaching starts from the inside and moves out.

Having the vision of our own worth and capability (and that of others) is an essential prerequisite to coaching. As you work through the following chapters, we hope you will discover that the greatest application of coaching will be for you, personally. We sometimes forget that we are our biggest advocates and our greatest consumers of coaching. The way you talk to yourself—the way you coach yourself—will enhance your own level of play in any endeavor you choose. Essentially, coaching starts from the inside and moves out. Bringing out another's talents should start bringing out your own talents. In order to become a good coaching partner, you need to develop the ability to coach yourself through new opportunities, challenges, and adversity. You must also be coachable and open to help from others who desire to support and serve you as a coach.

> Helen Keller was once asked by a reporter, "What can be worse than being blind?" She replied, "Having eyes to see but no vision."

To be the best you can be in today's demanding world, you will need coaches, facilitators, and mentors in your life.

We encourage you to find these partners. Appreciate them and invite them into your life because coaching, first and foremost, must be a shared learning experience. Dialogue isn't coaching if it doesn't enhance knowledge and perspective.

> The key is to act early, when you first see a coaching moment, so that others can choose to act while the information is current.

The great Chinese philosopher Lao Tzu said, "He who knows others is wise. He who knows himself is enlightened."

We hope that as you read this book, you will catch the "synergistic coaching spirit" and be able to achieve the benefits that come from good coaching relationships.

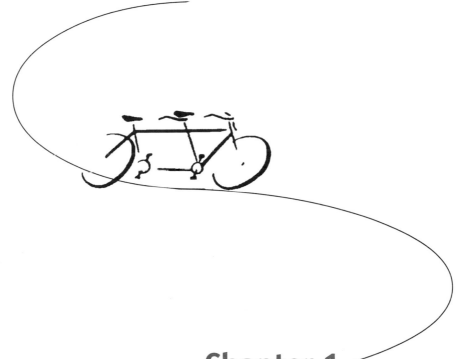

Chapter 1
Win-Win Partnerships

**(or life is about learning and
not being perfect)**

Life is About Learning—Not Being Perfect

Life is About Learning—
Not Being Perfect

It's about waking up each morning
knowing there is still something
left to discover about yourself
and the world around you
and that you still have a chance
to make a difference in both

Its about better
being better
doing better
a little bit at a time
with each decision and action
day by day
moment to moment
or in quantum leaps
that take your breath away

It's about hope
that tomorrow does not have to be
the same as today or yesterday
because you have a roadmap
created when history collides with
vision

It's about making mistakes
and seeing them as lessons
opportunities for growth
invitation to change
valuable chapters in your
lifelong education
whose debt you repay
by sharing those learnings

It's about being tolerant
and forgiving of yourself
and the other
less-than-perfect beings
who touch your life

You know some things in life
are so easy to say
yet, so hard to grasp
even more difficult to live
one of them is the fact that

Life is about learning—
not being perfect

© 1995 lydia frances
williams*

* **LFW Enterprises, P.O. Box 370234, Denver, Colorado 80237-0234, (303) 750-1040, (303)727-4889 (fax)**

Chapter 1
Win-Win Partnerships

Why Do We Need Partnerships in the First Place?

The ability to connect with others is so vital to modern life and our success as individuals. Large institutions and small teams alike depend on people being able to connect and open up with each other. If we can share what we are thinking, without being abrupt or presumptuous, we can chart a successful future, solve the problems we face, and achieve common ground. It is essential that we do more than express, advocate, and argue our own special interests. We can move forward if we learn to connect successfully and let go of our pre-formed solutions, work for consensus, and move as one.

We need to listen, learn, and understand what others think and need if we are to achieve synergy and grow.

A learning partnership is more than simply being personable, humorous, entertaining, and outgoing. It is much more than being controlling and autocratic with others. Certainly, it is more than ignoring or saying nothing when an opportunity presents itself for learning and change. We will describe in this book how to bridge to a new level—a level that will help us learn to grow together, to adapt, and cope with life's challenges in order to find joy and success in achieving our destiny.

A partnership means a quality relationship— one that is not based on mechanical or thoughtless compromise or the ability to charm or con others into doing things our way.

We all know that life isn't getting any less challenging or exciting. Life isn't getting any simpler. People are living longer and there are more opportunities. There are certainly not any less pressures living in today's environment. In a world of the "virtual" office and busy schedules, it is possible to go days without actually talking to anyone face-to-face, thanks to e-mail, voicemail and the Internet. Yet, we are faced with daily opportunities, problems, decisions, and agreements that need to be worked out through honest and direct communications with a whole host of co-workers, customers, suppliers, family members, friends, and instructors.

The reality is—partnerships are on the endangered species list. You don't have to look very hard to find evidence that everyone could try a little harder to work things out. The divorce rate still hovers around 50 percent, and the number of currently divorced persons has quadrupled since 1970. There is gridlock in Washington. Many workers continue to attribute work place dissatisfaction to poor relationships with supervisors and co-workers. Unfortunately, the work place today is one of the more likely places where people are killed or experience violence. While society needs diversity, there is far too much racial tension, generational tension, gender tensions, and personality tension. The need to build good working partner-ships won't ease up. Our future work force will face more challenges, get older, and become more diverse. Reconciling the conflicting needs of women, work, and families will require new thinking and solutions. It will take a lot of cooperation to integrate culturally diverse workers, provide educational opportunities to keep pace with rapid changes in technology, trade, and world politics. According to a 1996 census report (Special Study P23-191), the percentage of foreign-born people in the United States is at the highest level since before World War II. The future will bring constant streamlining, re-engineering, and

change. We may be on a collision course with destiny if we don't do more coaching and collaborating. In short, we may lose sight of the pathway to effective relationships with others.

As we journey through our lives, our careers, our education, our families, our friends, and numerous other relationships, we create a legacy and a pattern with other people. Even in brief, simple, or mechanical relationships, we create an imprint. Others take away a positive or negative impression of those relationships. Others can experience us as a short-term, one-way, win-lose partner; or as a long-term, two-way, win-win partner.

It is all a very subtle, almost thoughtless process. In fact, some of us rarely give it a moments thought. But regardless of our level of awareness, we are continually shaping and redesigning these relationships. Our relationships are constantly evolving and moving. They are developing or they are decaying. Who we are and what we do in a relationship will help determine if we are moving toward joint collaboration or destructive competition.

Our choices, beliefs, and actions determine whether we are creating allies or adversaries.

Creating good partnerships is a little like a balancing act. If you act unilaterally and seek only self interest, you alienate key players in your life. If you are totally dependent and helpless, you open up the possibility of being manipulated and controlled. It is easy to gravitate to these extremes. It is more challenging to form effective partnerships. We think that choosing to build a coaching relationship can make a positive difference.

Let's Look at a Real Example

Sid is an independent business woman who has had a fair amount of success and would certainly enjoy more. However, Sid came to us one day frustrated. In fact, she was more than frustrated. She was angry and burned out. We asked her to share what happened to make her feel this way. Like most of us, it was a busy day for Sid. She was focused on the task and the "business" and she was giving little if any thought to how she was connecting and communicating with others. As we soon learned, little thought and effort was going into building partnerships during the day.

Lets look close up at what we mean. Sid's first experience of the day was with her employees, five to be exact. She had noticed a bother-some trend with the office employees. Sid wanted a comfortable and relaxed work environment. But, some employees were going too far with blue jeans, tennis shoes, and T-shirts on an every-day basis. She said that she finally decided to "straighten things out." She called everyone together and simply told them that appearance was a big problem for her and the customers, and that she was unhappy with the way things were going. She said: "From now on, jeans and T-shirts are out!" She had made up her mind. There was no sense discussing the matter. It was her business and she was calling the shots and drawing a line. Some people felt a little embarrassed, and without comment, they went back to work with unresolved feelings about the matter. Sid said, "I got the cold shoulder all day. But tough. I am the boss and I should be able to say how I want this place to look." Sid had in fact just moved into an attractive new building, which leads us to her next encounter.

At 10:00 a.m. she had an on-site meeting with the City Landscape Inspector to review the property and release a sizable bond she had posted to move into the structure prior to the final inspection. We can't use the exact words she used, however, "Butt head bureaucrat" is close. She said the guy is a complete idiot. He is holding a cash bond because the plants are 10 inches apart instead of 6 inches as prescribed in Volume 3, Section 6, Paragraph A, Line 3 of the City landscape code. This blew Sid's top. Sid said, "I told him I wanted to meet with his boss and with the Mayor." Sid proclaimed in vain to the city representative about all the extra work, expense, and efforts to exceed municipal standards. It was true Sid has surpassed all expectations. But she failed to connect. She failed to effectively engage the dedicated public servant into an effective agreement. Sid let her emotions and thoughtlessness take control and dispatched the humble city inspector with anger. While it isn't all Sid's fault, she didn't do much to coach and connect in the meeting.

By afternoon, Sid was on a roll. She was in a groove. She was a force to be reconciled with.

At one o'clock in the afternoon, the advertising and media consultant shows up with recommendations for change to her company logo, brochures, and letterhead. From Sid's description, both people stumbled into the meeting. The consultant is skillful, clever, and dedicated. She is also blunt, not too sensitive, and a little egotistical. She is also new at freelance consulting. She started out with criticism and was a little too aggressive and personal for Sid. She failed to recognize that Sid's heart and soul had gone into the creation of the business. Sid froze up and became defensive. Sid had personally designed a lot of the documents on her desktop publishing computer. Sid's work was good, but the consultant had a microscope and pointed out a number of legitimate concerns. Here was an opportunity for collaboration and synergy. Instead what came out was frustration and hostility. There was a potential for a partnership. Sid could have been a very helpful coach for the consultant and vice versa. The consultant could have learned about the blind spot in her style. She didn't mean to hurt Sid's feelings. Instead of learning and growing, they ended the meeting in a cold, awkward way. There was no yelling and screaming, just an unproductive stalemate and rejection of potentially valuable ideas. In Sid's mind, she was saying, "Where does she get off on criticizing my hard work. Doesn't she realize that I have had other financial priorities in the past? Why doesn't she appreciate some of the good things I've done and recognize how far I have come as an amateur?" Instead of coaching, Sid holds it in. She silently resolves never to use the consultant's services again. A possible alliance quietly goes down the tube.

By now, Sid is fit to be tied. Her blood pressure is up. Her migraine is back, and to top it all, an insurance sales person is next on the agenda. The chance of creating a partnership is about as good as a lasting peace in the Balkans. Sid was completely closed to new ideas. She is suspicious of his claims. Consequently he moves into more of a classical sales approach. It is true, his plan is better than Sid's current one but both parties get tied in knots, both become defensive and resistant. Neither want to help, and both silently hope the meeting will end soon. Another emerging partnership goes down in flames.

Sid is exhausted, hurt, angry, and depressed about the day. She goes home early, crawls into her favorite chair, and checks out for the evening. She seems to be watching the tube but her thoughts are about her day from "hell." Her family and friends don't know what to say. They all recognize the dilemma and they just try to back off and give her some space. They are not quite sure how to help, and Sid isn't quite sure how to approach it differently.

In short, Sid lets things get to her. The events controlled her thoughts and behaviors. She didn't think through it, use her skills, and step back and try to see where things were headed. She got into a viscous cycle, assumptions were made, egos clashed and competitiveness entered the picture. Struggle for control emerged and defenses were ignited.

None of this was necessary. Hopefully you don't have many days that are a complete disaster like Sid's. How many times have we fallen short in our efforts to take our interactions and relationships to a higher plane and get things moving on the high road. Not all confrontations can be avoided. We have to be flexible sometimes. We need to fight and compete in some situations. But more often than not, opportunities for consensus, synergy, and collaboration go right by us. We often don't recognize the signals. We may not know what to say to get things moving in a positive direction. Sometimes we are impatient. We want the other party to come around, right now, to our way of thinking. We want things to be perfect and we want it fast. We want it our way. Sure we can compromise. We can be flexible, just as long as it agrees with our beliefs and desires.

You really do have options. You can create partnerships—coaching partnerships—if you are willing to try. If you are willing to free yourself up from a few old beliefs and practices.

Ultimately we can try and change the world around us, our environment, our circumstances. We can work hard, run fast, yell, scream, and cry, but no matter how hard we work or run, no matter how hard we fight or flee, there will always be some pain, some inequity, some unfairness, some sorrow. It seems that no matter how good science gets, there is always some world hunger. No matter how well we learn to understand the immune systems, we are always faced with new virus strains and diseases. We have learned how we can kill off the rain forests but we haven't learned how to kill off the common, everyday fly, cure colds, or grow hair.

You do have choices.

It seems to us that the challenge is how can we partner up with those around us so that we can learn to live successfully with challenges, enhance our own existence, and improve ourselves.

It seems to us that too much energy is focused on mammoth efforts like improving society, organizations , and institutions. It is a point that is difficult for a lot of us to see. Over and over again, we try to tackle the huge problems in our lives and in our organizations. We want to challenge corporate policies and corporate decisions.

Kahlil Gibran has said: "When we turn to one another for counsel, we reduce the number of our enemies."

We believe that job one is to develop and learn to live in our organizations and institutions. We need to learn how to grow and change at a personal and interpersonal level. Once we have a better handle and better mastery of our own personal change and growth, we can then focus more of our attention on the larger issues of society. But it is obviously balancing those extremes. We believe that as you think about partnerships, it is important to make a choice to live and enjoy, even though the turmoil is occurring around you. We can't and shouldn't try to force change. What we are suggesting is that we try to become attentive, responsible facilitators for our own growth, and to assist and promote our partners who impact our lives greatly in a positive way.

George Bernard Shaw captured this with the following thought, "I'm not a teacher— only a fellow traveler of whom you asked the way. I pointed ahead—ahead of myself as well as you."

After thinking about the idea of coaching and partnering, Sid tried again. She met with her staff and engaged them in open and constructive dialogue and worked out some practical solutions. Sid spent a half hour on the phone with her media consultant and they listened and gave each other some constructive feedback and decided they really could help each other. They began to build a symbiotic relationship. Sid met with the city bureaucrat three more times and created a positive relationship. In fact, he became a key contact and referred Sid some business from the city. The sales person, however, was deeply offended. He never returned Sid's calls. A potentially productive relationship dimmed and faded away. It isn't perfect but three out of four isn't too bad. Sid ended up living a little better. She decided to take a risk and open up to others.

In our line of work we run into people like Sid constantly. For example, Sandy and Delores are locked into a partnership that is an incredibly stressful situation. It is producing serious physical symptoms and side affects for Sandy. Delores rarely gives Sandy any recognition or appreciates her efforts. Delores is a micro-manager and does a poor job of communicating her expectations. She wants a lot from Sandy but she is not a synergistic coach. Sandy is aggressively looking for a change.

Nancy is a supplier for Don. But Don is constantly irritated by the way Nancy comes across. Yet they have not effectively surfaced and dealt with the issues. It has been going on for two years. Now both are emotional about it. Nancy is surprised and devastated. She wants to know more about her blind spots but struggles with the way Don is communicating.

Dave and Erin have worked together for over 15 years. One at corporation headquarters and the other in charge of field operations. They are different in style and philosophy. Yet Erin has a blind spot—she's a real numbers and detail person, but she isn't helping give the leadership that is needed in the field. Dave is frustrated and ready to retire early because he can't get through. He feels like giving up and is struggling to figure out a way to rebuild a relationship. To be more accurate, he is not sure how to build a relationship for the first time with Erin.

Linda is another example. She is the new leader of a Neighborhood Association, and she is about go ballistic. She and Bob, a resident and member, are not

seeing eye to eye on some policy issues. Now it has become heated. Bob is talking to his legal advisor and Linda is shopping for a home 25 miles away from Bob. Have they talked? Yes. Have the communicated? No.

They are missing each other. Both have ears to hear but they are not listening. It is becoming very painful and costly. Now the neighborhood is taking sides. Bob and Linda are taking it personally. They are not using a process. They are in a hopeless downward spiral.

Keep in mind that when you are throwing dirt, you are losing ground.

All of these people could be in powerful alliances rather than adversaries. They could learn to be a coach and resource for each other. Most of these people are in either the "say nothing" avoidance mode or in the "explode and rip a new one" mode. They don't know the rules of engagement. Far too many of these relationships are on "life support." Some of them will always be on life support. Some of them can come back. All of them are worth the effort. Any promising idea, skill, or value would help improve their physical, emotional or economic quality of life. Someone has to start a more productive process. Someone in the partnership has to get it going. When do you speak? When do you remain silent? When do you ask? When do you tell? What principles and values do you strive for? As you read further, we believe you will find answers to these and many other questions to help renew your key partnerships. The renewal process is something that you won't be able to control exactly. We have only limited control in what happens to our own bodies. We have no control over the weather, other drivers on the road, or the pilot who flies the airplane. In a relationship, you need to be an effective half. You need to exercise your coaching stewardship and not be a passenger strapped hopelessly in a seat belt as the plane goes down in flames. You need to struggle, learn, and try gracefully to steer a productive course.

Control is nothing more than a mirage.

The whole intent of a good partnership boils down to:

1) **Responsibility**—Getting each member to accept responsibility for challenges and opportunities and not "duck" out.

2) **Integrity**—Getting members to do what they say and be true to their commitment.

3) **Openness**—Saying what's on one's mind in a constructive, non-hurtful way.

4) **Synergy**—Combining the talents and creativity in the partnership to find new ideas and ways of achieving goals.

Chapter 2
Synergistic Coaching:
Your Values are Showing!

(or your actions tell people
what you value)

Chapter 2
Synergistic Coaching: Your Values are Showing!

Go Beyond Actions and Behaviors

Modern organizations, and in fact, society, are full of positive-sounding actions and prescriptions guaranteed to unleash productivity, quality, and satisfaction. These prescriptions include ideas like: collaboration, empowerment, paradigm shifting, partnering, re-engineering, and teamwork. Yet, would you readily admit (even to yourself) that your actions are often inconsistent with the intent of these concepts? These concepts are good and needed, but our self-serving bias may prevent us from recognizing that our actions may not reflect our intentions. This blind spot may hold you back and keep you from moving to a more effective level of coaching, to a synergistic level.

Who doesn't want to believe that they are effective and cooperative?

Our experience with teams is that none of them felt they lacked teamwork until teamwork was more specifically described and examined. Who would admit that they do not act with integrity, trustworthiness, honesty, sincerity, empathy, respect, humility, openness, and flexibility? Isn't it true that the meaning of these behaviors is "in the eye of the beholder?"

You must also work on your values so the behaviors will naturally occur.

Focusing on actions or behaviors is not sufficient for those who want to move with others through the learning process. You cannot force them, because our true nature will show under pressure.

How individual actions are interpreted may vary. For example, is asking questions during a coaching discussion, while not wanting to relinquish control over the desired outcome or plan, true collaboration? We think not, yet some may feel that this is collaboration. Can you enter into a partnership and withhold information that others need to make informed choices? Our answer is no; yet, others feel that limited partnerships are a possibility.

We have fallen into this same trap by espousing the virtues of synergistic coaching, only to find that, by our definition, few interactions are truly collaborative. Yet the paradox is that most coaches feel they are synergistic when in fact they are not. Some people mistakenly view our coaching model as a clever way to get the coach's ideas implemented and to "manipulate" the thinking of others. With a wrong set of values, the actions taken in each of the eight steps of our model could be used inappropriately to gain more, not less control—to manipulate, not collaborate.

Value-based coaching is a way of being: "to help" instead of "to win" at the expense of others.

A more effective approach is to examine the "root values" that give meaning to your actions. Through an understanding of which values you are living, meaning and substance are given to collaboration, partnership, and synergy.

Coaching discussions are the true amphitheater where your values are on display.

Chris Argyris distinguishes between your **espoused theory** and your **theory in use**. Coaching discussions are the arena where you cannot hide from your theory in use. In this arena, visible evidence is provided as to your core, or root, values. Your true nature will reveal itself because it is very difficult, if not impossible, to act contrary to your root values in critical situations.

Values that Support Learning and Synergy

Values are like relatives: we all have them. The key is to understand how they affect your relationships with others. To be an effective coaching partner requires a mental shift to see your role as a resource or catalyst to help others achieve what they decide is best for them—to collaborate. We see two extremes: those values that lead to collaborative behaviors, and those that lead to command and control behaviors. Our focus here is on the values that lead to collaborative behaviors which are the bedrock of synergistic coaching. Our use of the term *values* does not exclude other terms, such as *principles, beliefs, virtues,* or *character* that the reader may be more comfortable with.

Three Viewpoints

"I"
"You"
"Us"

As a coach, aspiring to foster synergistic behavior, you live out sets of values, "**I**"; about others, "**you**"; values about partnerships, "**us.**" What follows is a selective description of these three "core" dimensions of a synergistic viewpoint. These three vistas represent a refinement of our observations, discussions, and research with effective coaches we have known. We encourage you to expand and individualize them to give them personal meaning.

Level One: Four Core Values About Me

I Am Secure

Values concerning yourself are the most fundamental drivers and greatly influence the values you hold about others. You must be comfortable at the inner, or self-level, before you can be effective at the "us" (partner) level. Do you appreciate and value your own identity and individualism? Do you like yourself, and are you comfortable with who you are? Secure people act with humility, dignity, and modesty. They are not self-centered. They have nothing to prove. *One client looks for people who are intellectually honest*—will they do the right thing? For secure people, success is not defined as material wealth, fame, power, or social status, but it offers both fulfillment and happiness as they invest themselves in worthwhile pursuits.

This doesn't mean that secure people are not always striving to be better; it is just not at the expense of others. For them to be winners, others don't have to be losers. They are capable of seeing other's victories as wins, and are secure enough to celebrate those wins. They can dim their headlights and allow others to shine.

Core values are ideals to strive toward. We are constantly working on living these values, knowing that perfection is an impossible goal—it is a work in progress. The quality of our relationships are based on others' perceptions that our actions are aligned with core partnership values.

Secure people act with humility, dignity, and modesty.

In the final days of his second term, Harry Truman summarized his accomplishments by saying, "I have tried to give it everything that was in me."

Each person is unique and this uniqueness has value. Therefore, if I am comfortable with myself and can be comfortable that others also are unique and valued, then my goal is to be the best that I can so that my partners will do likewise.

Insecure people are filled with anxiety and doubt; they live in a world of competition, constantly trying to prove to themselves and others that they are worthwhile. This can be manifest in any number of ways: always wanting to be in control, never recognizing others' accomplishments, always affirming how good and wonderful they are, monopolizing the conversation with their agenda. In other words, they are real bores. No one likes a braggart. No one is attracted to arrogance, or admires presumptuousness.

"Best" doesn't mean financial success or winning but the peace of mind and personal satisfaction that you did your best.

Security means knowing what your strengths and weaknesses are and playing to your strengths while letting others develop their own. You feel comfortable being yourself, not what others expect you to be, which results in an inner strength and self-confidence. The strengths of others are not threats, they are assets. Yet true confidence is displayed by letting go, not by taking over. Many can remember thinking how confident a person was, only on reflection to find them loud, rude, controlling, or insensitive. They were at center stage, unwilling to listen or uninterested in others' ideas.

If you believe in your security, then you accept others and don't try to make them like you. Their uniqueness is valued. You play to your strengths and compete against your standards, not against others. You control only what you can control—yourself. This confidence allow you to be prepared mentally, morally, and spiritually. Others will be comfortable when they are around you; fear will be minimized.

We have mentioned Harry Truman, and although many may argue with his policy about the atomic bomb, or his political stance, few would question his sense of personal security. When faced with contrary advice during crucial turning points in our country's history, he believed in himself, yet showed humility: "What's wrong with being an average man?" Those in the White House who saw him daily, at all hours, and often under extremely trying circumstances, stated: "He seemed to have some kind of added inner balance mechanism that held him steady through nearly anything, enabling him not only to uphold the fearful responsibilities of his office and keep a killing schedule…it was a level of equanimity that at times left those around him hugely amused and even more fond of him."

Similar illustrations of those who are secure with themselves could be cited. As one final example, Abraham Lincoln overcame feelings of insecurity and lack of self-esteem to be ranked consistently as the greatest President. "He was open, civil, tolerant, and fair, and he maintained a respect for the dignity of all people at all times.

I Am An Optimist

Optimists anticipate positive outcomes; when others see problems, they see opportunities. In the face of adversity or disappointment, they look for the silver lining. When options appear blocked, optimists have the determination to find another way. They move ahead, even though rocks and barriers are in the path. They aren't blindly ignorant of realities, but try to make the most of any situation. True optimists do not overestimate the upside, but they look until they find the upside potential, regardless of its size. Optimists do not exaggerate the possibilities, but choose to discover the hope inherent in any situation.

Respect for others starts with a respect for self.

"Lincoln's attitude and behavior as President of the United States essentially characterized the process that symbolizes acceptable and decent relation-ships among human beings."

The book *Man's Search For Meaning* recounts chilling experiences of Viktor Frankl, a noted psychiatrist, who was imprisoned at Auschwitz and other concentration camps in World War II. Frankl concluded that some prisoners not only survived the horrifying conditions but were able to grow in the process. We agree with Frankl and believe that those who can find meaning, those who can find a lesson to learn, can grow in life.

People who are pessimistic, negative, or apathetic no longer see the purpose in their lives and have lost interest in the lives of others. A true coaching partner makes the choice to be interested in others, no matter what the situation. The optimist chooses to look for the growth opportunity, seeing it as the key to overcoming big problems and trivial day-to-day issues. Search for reasons to be helpful. Don't expect hope to automatically jump out at you. It is a skill or talent to develop.

According to Victor Frankl, as much as one third of the population has a critical deficit of hope and meaning. This poisons the partnership and coaching process. When you give up, or become negative and cynical, you "run into the wire." This phrase describes a popular form of prisoner suicide: touching the electrically charged wire fence. An optimist fosters a synergistic partnership where members are charged up internally and the negative voltage of despair or negativity remains low.

I Am A Teacher

Regardless of your employment status or job title, helping others learn and grow has its own reward. We have not used the term *mentor* because sometimes this implies advancement, someone in higher authority, and is organization-specific. A teacher can be a friend, an associate, your leader, or a significant other. We don't use the term to imply a job (e.g., school teacher), but rather the value of helping others learn. The key is that you find it intrinsically rewarding to help others grow. Development of others can be part of a manager's job description, but that description doesn't capture the activities and satisfaction that come from being a teacher.

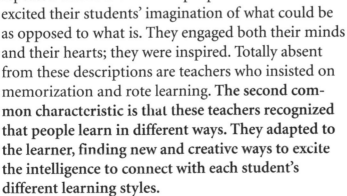

All of us have had the good fortune of interacting with at least one special teacher during our education. Even the NFL (National Football League) presents an award from one of the superstars to a teacher he felt most impacted his life. When good teachers are described, a repeated theme is that these people excited their students' imagination of what could be as opposed to what is. They engaged both their minds and their hearts; they were inspired. Totally absent from these descriptions are teachers who insisted on memorization and rote learning. **The second common characteristic is that these teachers recognized that people learn in different ways. They adapted to the learner, finding new and creative ways to excite the intelligence to connect with each student's different learning styles.**

> Albert Einstein once said,
> "Imagination is more important
> than knowledge."

But what impact do teachers have on life or career success?

A Senior Vice President, President, and CEO of a major corporation recently concluded that each could point to three people who were influential in their success. For each, the three were different people, but they had much in common: they were not people in power, or upper managers, or always their direct manager; nor did they advance much beyond their current level in the organization. What they did do was spend time teaching these people, connecting to their imagination of what could be, what they were capable of, and what it would take to achieve these ends. The interesting conclusion was that they received no apparent monetary or organizational reward for spending this time but found their reward in the teaching process itself.

So what about you?

What would you miss most if the rest of your life was to be spent in isolation on a remote island? If toward the top of your list of answers is, "the chance to interact and help the people I come in contact with," congratulations! Despite what you may think, you are a teacher. To be a teacher represents a significant paradigm shift: helping others achieve their own goals versus imposing or selling solutions that meet your goals. Your rewards are in the growth and success of others. You don't have to get your way or solve their problems to be a successful partner.

I Am Just

A coaching partner always strives to be fair, just, and patient. Rather than conformity to harsh rules, justice is based on reason and logic. Synergistic coaching seeks out the best information, facts, and objectivity to form plans.

Disraeli once said, "Justice is truth in action."

When you arc just, you believe in being treated fairly and in treating others fairly. Striving to be impartial and restrain personal biases, the just coach shows due appreciation and advocates appropriate consequences. Justice is based on appropriate measures, responses, and actions.

Justice and fairness are very subjective ideas. You will forever hear the cry that "life just isn't fair." Nevertheless, when people see you espouse justice and act accordingly, you build a base of positive influence. Others will trust you.

Fair is a place you take your pig

Dennis Green, head coach of the Minnesota Vikings, sums it up: "My general rule, which I have followed throughout my coaching career, is that everyone doesn't necessarily get treated the same way, because I'm not sure that's possible. But everyone has to be treated fairly."

Level Two: Four Core Values About Others

"When I asked Peter to tell me about Paul, I found out more about Peter than I did Paul."

In discussing your views about others, an interesting phenomenon exists. The values you hold about others are also the values you hold about yourself. You ascribe to others those characteristics you embody. To hold the following values about others also means you hold these same values about yourself.

You Are Valuable

Looking at others this way means you believe the total person is worthwhile: values, skills, and distinctive qualities. This goes beyond the popular term of "valuing diversity," which implies valuing others only because they are different. Finding others valuable, period, means that they have legitimate mental, physical, and emotional assets to contribute, regardless of how different or similar you and they are. It also means that you don't have a corner on good ideas, broader perspectives, intelligence, or relevant experiences.

Easier said than done. The Danzigers, in an insightful manual, explore the concept that we all have a "Life Pattern," caused by a single fixed belief which makes you better than others, allows you to win or puts you on top of others. The culprit is the word "more." Each of us believes that "I am more X," where "X" can be any belief about yourself, such as, "I am more intelligent, organized, sensitive, responsible, creative, prompt, truthful, detailed, courteous, etc." This belief causes four problems in our relationships with others:

1. Others are less "X," and it's not okay with me that they are less.
2. I must keep being more "X"; I must always be "X."
3. I am separate from others who lack "X."
4. Others should notice that I am more "X" and appreciate it.

A belief in being more "X" can cause a host of negative thoughts and behaviors; e.g., criticism, judgment, separateness, distorted perceptions of worth, conflicts, negative thoughts about others and yourself, stress, and tensions.

What to do? The good news is that everyone has these Life Patterns, they are not always serious, and if they are detrimental they can be changed. The Danzigers suggest first identifying those critical "more X" beliefs and then restating your beliefs so that both you and others will be right. For example, you can learn from the X quality in each other. It is okay for you to be X because Shawntell is unique in the area of Y. Restating and then implementing these ideas are the keys to change.

If you believe that others have legitimate ideas and feelings, and respect their differences, you will recognize that differences of opinion are good and that others' perceptions/ideas have merit and deserve consideration. You will seek opposing views that challenge your thinking. Even though you may believe you are more capable in certain areas, you value others and understand their unique contributions.

You Are Principled

There are certain natural laws that guide behavior. These are held as right and not to be violated; they are like the ten commandments of coaching. Although ten seems a lot for us mere mortals, five commandments govern personal and interpersonal behavior and are the compass that defines "doing what is right."

Five commandments govern principled behavior:

1. Self-determining
2. Excelling
3 Adaptable
4. Responsible
5. Respectful

1. Self-determining. Others determine their own fate. In the final analysis, the only thing we can control is ourselves. Others' behavior is a decision, based on informed choice, not their condition. As Chris Argyris states, "One of the central findings of our research is that people reason differently when they think about a problem simply to understand it than when they intend to take action. If the objective is to discover and understand, then there is plenty of time for elegant and comprehensive understanding." Others seek out and desire descriptive/clear information and data for their consideration. The corollary is that others seek and desire constant feedback from you to confirm or change the decisions that affect their lives. When it helps the other person discover and reach understanding and is not presented as a command, the feedback will be listened to and considered. Choice, time, and space are important factors. How and the speed at which a person processes confirming or new data are up to the individual. This process cannot be accelerated. In addition to seeking feedback from others, people need to be inquisitive and test their assumptions against the realities of the situation.

Without choice, people feel constrained and not in control.

Go Slow
Obstacles
Ahead

2. Excelling. This principle goes beyond doing your best to excelling at those things you find worthwhile. It includes the concepts of quality and continuous improvement; excellence is a moving target. Who among our readers can admit that they set out to do a poor job, to play a lousy game of tennis, to really screw up a presentation? We may never reach our targets, yet we all strive to excel, hoping to be better tomorrow than we are today. Helping others have realistic targets and directing their energies to pursue the right endeavors are the challenges.

3. Adaptable. Change is a given, and the only way to not stagnate is to be adaptable, flexible, and open-minded. People will always consider alternatives. How many of our readers are in the same career with the same organization they were with five years ago? The belief in a job for life or staying with one organization until retirement are equations for emotional stress.

> **When working with others, start by assuming that they are open-minded.**

A central tenant of synergistic coaching is to help others consider alternatives. Although the word *proactive* is often overused, in this context, it has meaning: the people you interact with would rather act than be acted upon. Looking back on your life, your versatility in meeting changing conditions may surprise you.

4. Responsible. The principled mature person is responsible and acts responsibly. "He made me do it," or "Certain events contributed to the condition," represent the excuses the less mature person falls back on when seeking forgiveness. How refreshing to hear, "I was wrong," "I was responsible," or, "I am accountable." People are much more

The Devil made me do it!

Side notes:

The rapid and constant societal and organizational changes as we move into a new century make adaptability a prerequisite for sanity.

This principle alone sets the human race apart from other species, especially those facing extinction.

If not impossible, it is very difficult to have a productive discussion with another person unless both parties are responsible for their actions.

willing to accept the current condition and move on when others are accountable for their actions. The irresponsible partner lives in the past, seeking to place blame. The responsible partner assesses the situation and moves on without blaming others.

The research of Fisher and Ury, developed at the Harvard Negotiation Project, led to the conclusion that you can be both respectful of the person and tough on the issues.

5. Respectful. It is possible to be polite, civil, and courteous to others rather than rude or antagonistic. Mutual respect for one another does not mean that one person has to give in. To accomplish this, the parties in a negotiation must separate the people from the problem, focus on interests not positions, generate a variety of possibilities before deciding what to do, and insist that the result be based on some objective standard. Then figuratively, if not literally, the participants should come to see themselves as working side by side, attacking the problem, not each other.

You Are Trustworthy

Trust is a two-way street: the coach has to take the first step and believe the other person is trustworthy.

For other people to be worthy of your trust, you must feel their motives are pure—not selfish, devious, or partisan. When put to the true test, they will respond reasonably. Viewing others as trustworthy means you are willing to take risks with them and be vulnerable. Few would argue that trust is a fundamental ingredient or lubricant, an unavoidable dimension of productive social interaction. Yet what ingredients contribute to another person being viewed as trustworthy? After an extensive literature review, Mayer, Davis, and Schoorman synthesize these into three characteristics of the other person— ability, benevolence, and integrity—to explain a major portion of trustworthiness. **Ability** is that group of skills, expertise, or competencies that suggest an individual may be trusted to perform a task. Clearly we

Ability
—
Benevolence
—
Integrity

would not see a competent banker as a trustworthy surgeon. **Benevolence** is the extent to which a person is seen as wanting good things for the partnership. **Integrity** is the perception that the other person adheres to a set of principles that the coach finds acceptable. Benevolence and integrity delve into the other person's intentions and motives. If you believe others are principled, as previously discussed, you are a long way toward meeting the characteristics of a synergistic coach.

You Are Safe

Everyone needs a sense of security, to feel out of harm's way, invulnerable. It is the strongest driver of actions. People strive toward meeting this need by seeking to control those things that affect them. But in a world of rapid and constant change, control is

We can never own security; at best, we can rent it for a while.

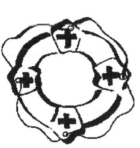

difficult. Nevertheless, the need to feel safe and secure remains intense. As Connor notes, it is not the velocity of change that is the issue. Our lives are the most effective and efficient (safe and secure, in other words) when we are moving at a speed that allows us to appropriately assimilate the changes we face. Major changes often equate to feeling at a loss to control the environment. How can a coaching partner help regain a sense of control?

People are most comfortable (safe) when they can influence what happens to them, the ability to influence is largely dependent on being prepared for what will happen.

Coaching deals with the future. A coaching partner helps others clarify current, as well as future, expectations.

Preparedness is, to a great extent, contingent on establishing accurate expectations about the future. People feel in control of their lives when their expectations match what they perceive to be actually occurring. Once these expectations are recognized, the coaching partners can define appropriate actions. Through the process of clarifying expectations and mutual planning to meet these expectations, the coach both recognizes and validates the other person's needs for safety and security.

Level Three: Four Core Values About "Us" (Partnerships)

We Are Allies

On the basis of their research, Cohen and Bradford concluded: Effective influence begins with the way you think about those you want to influence. You have won half the battle when you can see each person, no matter how stubborn, as a potential strategic partner.

The strongest determiner of how you approach your conversations with others is your mental frame of mind. How do you view each other? Allies seek out ways to help one another; competitors seek out ways to win. Allies believe that the pie is growing, competitors see the pie as fixed—for me to get a bigger piece means your piece will be smaller. From the coach's perspective, the most valuable mindset is "How can I help you reach your goals?" Unfortunately, too many times coaches view their role not as helper or enabler but gatekeeper. At the end of any conversation, the acid test is whether it has been helpful.

We Are Vulnerable

One way to keep from being vulnerable is to mold your conversation into "politically correct" terms. Believing you might hurt, offend, put off, or insult others, you modify your speech so that only artificial things are said or that issues/topics are framed with an overly positive spin. The problem is you may have never tested your assumptions. You made a choice for the other person and altered your beliefs into phrases that are positive. The solution is easy to state but hard to live by: discuss the undiscussable. Chris Argyris documented that the main contributor to "double-loop" learning is a willingness to discuss the undiscussable. In repeated testing where people divided their conversations with others into two columns—those things said and those things unsaid—a more open, free flow of information was created when the "things unsaid" were discussed in a fashion that tested the validity of these assumptions.

To be vulnerable means to be open, to share, to be unprotected.

For example, something unsaid might be that the other person will find any reactions contrary to their proposals as argumentative; therefore, you need to state everything positively or say nothing at all. Openly discussing this assumption allows the two people to test its validity; not discussing it robs the conversation of much depth and the chance for an open exploration of alternatives. Taking the risk requires both parties to be vulnerable.

We Are Learners

In *The Fifth Discipline*, Peter Senge states, "Learning organizations are possible because, deep down, we are all learners." This refers to the natural inquisitiveness in all of us. Although Senge is first to admit that the learning organization is not a wide-spread phenomenon, it can be focused on a much smaller scale, me and you. On this level Senge sheds some light on one of the five dimensions, Personal Mastery:

We believe you can't have a learning organization until you have created one-to-one learning relationships!

"Personal mastery is the discipline of continually clarifying and deepening our personal vision, of focusing our energies, of developing patience, and of seeing reality objectively."

Few organizations encourage the growth of their people in this manner; however, coaching partnerships can achieve a state where individuals learn from each other. When you interact with others, one of your first thoughts should be, "What can I learn?" or "How will I grow from this discussion?" Do you allow each other to experiment, and are you tolerant of inevitable mistakes? Do you take the risk to try new things and learn from your mistakes? Living the principles held about you and your coaching partner requires you mutually and individually to become

personal master-learners. What a wonderful foundation for a coaching interaction when both parties enter into the discussion ready to explore, to learn, to grow, instead of to defend, deny, argue, debate. You relish the opportunities to expand your thinking, hear new ideas, learn new things. You want to make a difference. You want to have an affect on someone or something so your life has an extrinsic meaning beyond the time you spend. This is a very powerful driver, and it can cause you to be more forceful in your attempts to influence one another in a helpful way.

If you believe in personal mastery, then stewardship of resources is important. The term *resources* is expansive; it includes everything you come in contact with. Are the resources better because you were involved with them? Others have valuable insight that you can leverage for learning and growth. How can you be coached? Your actions are visible illustrations of your desire to learn and grow, your willingness to show your humanness and imperfection. You are provisional, open, surprised, because you don't know it all.

For you, perfection is a journey, not an end.

We Are Reliable

Reliability is a state of being. It constitutes the "foundation" value in a win-win partnership, just like a stabilizer on an airplane, or the keel on a boat. When partners do what they say, a feeling of predictability is created. When coaching partners act on their stated intentions, stability results. This positive form of predictability does not destroy flexibility, spontaneity, or creativity. Predictability is a key to the illusive concept of trust and trustworthiness.

Reliability does not suggest that you can't change your mind. It simply means that coaching precedes the act. Reliability means that when action is called for, it will happen every time. In a reliable partnership, the needs of the other are not ignored. Reliable action stems from shared interests, not self-interest.

> Too often, the right thing gets said and the wrong thing gets done.

Walking the talk is not easy. If you are unreliable or inconsistent, your credibility takes a nose-dive. Keeping your commitments and promises, on the other hand, builds credibility and dependability.

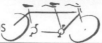
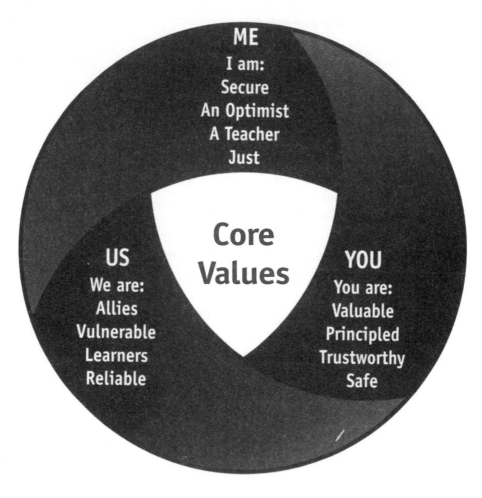

ME
I am:
Secure
An Optimist
A Teacher
Just

Core Values

US
We are:
Allies
Vulnerable
Learners
Reliable

YOU
You are:
Valuable
Principled
Trustworthy
Safe

Pathway to Collaboration

- ♦ Reciprocal trust/respect
- ♦ Discovery and understanding first; action second
- ♦ Advocacy in a way that invites inquiry and testing
- ♦ Generation of a variety of possibilities
- ♦ Working side by side attacking the issues, not each other
- ♦ Understanding and goals, not defending of positions
- ♦ A mutual question: How can I help you reach your goals?
- ♦ Ability to be coached

What are the Payoffs?

Two researchers asked a similar question: What are the likely outcomes of using different influence tactics? They compared various influence tactics used by subordinates, peer's, and bosses to the outcomes of resistance, compliance, and commitment. The influence tactics can be grouped into three categories:

Influence Tactics:

1. Collaboration/ consultation
2. Rational persuasion
3. Use of authority

1. **Collaboration/Consultation:**
    Building the other person's enthusiasm by appealing to his or her values, ideals, and/or aspirations. Seeking the other person's participation in planning a strategy or being willing to modify a proposal to respond to the other person's concerns.

2. **Rational persuasion:**
    Appealing to the other person's feeling of loyalty, and using logical arguments and factual evidence to persuade the other person that proposals or requests are worthwhile.

3. **Use of authority:**
    Using demands or threats, enlisting the aid or endorsement of other people, or claiming authority based on organization policies, rules, or traditions to influence the person to do what is wanted.

Outcomes:

1. Commitment
2. Compliance
3. Resistance

The research question explored was: What difference, if any, do these influence tactics have on the other person's feelings regarding the following three outcomes?:

1. **Commitment:**
    The other person agrees internally with an action or decision, is enthusiastic about it, and is likely to exercise initiative and demonstrate unusual effort and persistence in order to carry out the request successfully.

2. **Compliance:**
    The other person carries out the requested action but is apathetic rather than enthusiastic, makes only a minimal or average effort, and does not show any initiative.

3. **Resistance:**
    The other person opposes the requested action and tries to avoid carrying it out by refusing, arguing, delaying, or seeking to have the request nullified.

The data presented in the following chart are very clear: Collaboration/consultation produced significantly higher levels of commitment and significantly lower levels of compliance and resistance than the use of authority. Rational persuasion was middle range in producing commitment, compliance, and resistance.

Effects of Style on Influence

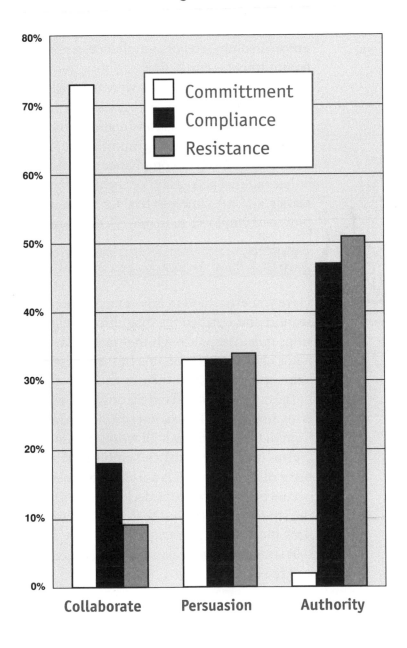

The use of power tactics or a one-way coaching discussion that relies on telling, or, attempting to sell, the other person on both the need for and direction of, the desired actions produces a high level of resistance, medium level of compliance, and low level of commitment—hardly a prescription for a learning environment. These results were true regardless of the direction of the influence: peer-to-peer influence based on collaboration/consultation produced significantly higher levels of commitment and significantly lower levels of compliance and resistance than either rational persuasion or the use of authority tactics, and the same was true for manager-to-employee or employee to manager collaboration.

The Tall Ships—A Concluding Thought

Have you ever stood in amazement at a harbor or seaport and watched the magnificent, tall clipper ships quietly slip through the water? Have you ever had a chance to ride on one of these magnificent ships and watch them silently, and almost effortlessly, harness the winds and cut through the rough seas. It is an amazing collaboration of wood, rope, and human talent to make it all work. It is an alliance that creates incredible speed and endurance. At the centerpiece of all this action is a unique partnership. It occurs between the ships deck and the mast. In fact, the strategic component that locks the mast to the deck is called the *partner*. It is the heavy, thick timber that strengthens the relationship between the ship and the mast.

Like the values, it is not very flashy. A lot of people probably wouldn't even notice that it is there because it doesn't get a lot of visibility, but it reinforces and ensures the performance of the ship. With the partner in place, the vessel can move forward at great speed, harness stiff wind, and take advantage of the harsh elements. Coaching values remind us a lot of these tall ships. The sails ride high and are very visible and telling, just like our behaviors. But it is our values that make up the core character. If we have a little slip or tear in the fabric of our behavior, it is our values and what others know that will keep our relationships afloat. Just like the *partners* on the tall ships, we probably don't talk about values a lot. But they are

In essence, the partner helps harness an apparent obstacle and turn it into a valuable resource.

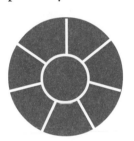 there silently making an enormous contribution for good or ill. Combined with the Coaching Model (see Chapter 5) you can truly put your relationships on the "leading edge" of life's exciting challenges.

Synergistic coaching values propel our relationships forward.

Chapter 3
What is Synergistic Coaching?

The effective coaching partner has the ability to be firm and fair to push a little at the right time, and yet be flexible at the appropriate moment.

The Coach

Chapter 3
What is Synergistic Coaching?

Covenantal Relationships

About 30 miles southwest of Grand Rapids, Michigan, close to the eastern shores of Lake Michigan, lies the small township of Zeeland. This rural community is known to few, except for those in the furniture manufacturing industry. Nestled on the outskirts of Zeeland is the world headquarters of Herman Miller, Inc., a furniture manufacturing company that was named one of Fortune magazine's ten "best managed" and "most innovative" companies. It was also chosen as one of the hundred best companies to work for in America.

Herman Miller, Inc. was formed by Mr. D.J. De Pree, in 1923. Later, D.J.'s son, Max, served as the company's chairman and CEO. Inheriting a coaching philosophy from his father, Max has generously shared his personal and corporate vision. He has done this by authoring two books: *Leadership is an Art* and *Leadership Jazz*. We highly recommend both of these books, especially for the rich blend of warmth and insights about learning relationships.

Covenantal Relationships

On page 51 of *Leadership is an Art*, De Pree introduces a term called "covenantal relationships." He states: "Covenantal relationships . . . induce freedom, not paralysis. A covenantal relationship rests on shared commitment to ideas, to issues, to values, and to goals. Words such as caring, warmth, and personal chemistry are certainly pertinent. Covenantal relationships are open to influence. They fill deep needs and they enable work to have meaning and to be fulfilling. They reflect unity and grace and poise. They are an expression of the sacred nature of relationships."

As we internalize the above statement and relate it to synergistic coaching, we catch the essence of a *mission* in our relationships. We sense that Max De Pree built one of the most successful companies in the world by being a coach who values partnerships. We believe that the alignment between mission and coaching skills creates success for them.

Over the years, we have learned that just because a person assumes the title of coach, that designation doesn't automatically translate to good coach. Just as with other roles, a huge difference can exist between one's competency and one's title or position. Businesses use the title of manager, although numerous managers daily demonstrate poor management skills. We also see parents and teachers who have those job titles, yet some have extremely poor parenting or teaching skills.

Coaching Is A Process, Not A Title

When we describe coaching, we do not mean a person or a job title. Coaching is not a noun. To us, coaching means a process: it is a verb. A verb suggests action and dynamics. It is something you can DO! It can be observed and learned by almost anyone, regardless of role, occupation, or calling in life.

Just because a person assumes the title of "coach," that designation doesn't automatically translate to "good coach."

It is just as appropriate for a team member to coach as it is for a leader to do so.

Over the years, the term coaching has been used in many contexts. In the 1500's, the term was frequently associated with the process of transporting or conveying. It was the coach that preceded the automobile and the taxi cab. In the 1800's, the term was used to refer to the tutoring process and to the training of athletes. In the 1900's, it became the job title for the leader of a team participating in sports. More recently, however, persons in many types of organizations have adopted this term to refer to effective communication, mentoring, superior leadership, and win/win interpersonal relationships.

The word process is critical to our definition of coaching. By this we mean how coaching is done. It is the operations, actions, or steps that bring about the end result.

A *PROCESS* is an ongoing movement, or a progression of steps to help prepare, treat or convert into something special (according to Webster).

The Essence of Coaching

The very essence of synergistic coaching is the process of creating effective dialogue promoting understanding. Effective dialogue between two people can lead to clear direction, amiable agreements, synergistic solutions, and creativity. These elements enable people to perform their roles with greater responsibility and enthusiasm. The net result for both partners is enhanced self-concepts, (who they think they are) as well as increased self-esteem (how they feel about who they think they are).

Coaching focuses on creating mutually helpful relationships between adults in all types of associations (businesses, marriages, families, schools, and government). Coaching can also be used in one-on-one and group interactions.

The coaching process is heart—warming because it helps people grow, learn, live, share, and sustain meaningful relationships. Essentially, coaching is a two-way process of constructively influencing human behavior.

Diving Even Deeper

At a deeper level, when we coach people, we are attempting to go directly to important topics. In a spirit of openness, we look for ways that we can help each other with challenges and obstacles. It takes skill, thought, and spirit to create quality, productive relationships with people who matter to us. Coaching seeks common ground and direction through open dialogue free of fear, intimidation, or control. In a coaching relationship, individuals share their reactions and viewpoints in an atmosphere of trust, as they reflect on choices about future behavior and agreements.

Coaches look for shared values, then align their behavior and actions with these values. Coaching means sharing knowledge and information in a non-threatening and supportive manner. As ideas are generated, effective communication skills are essential for the partners to learn from each other.

Coaching is not about getting the most out of a partnership; it is about getting the best from a partnership.

Coaching is not about rejection or blame. It is about continuous mutual improvement.

One of the central reasons people coach is to explain perceptions, talk about perceived expectations, and to achieve understanding so those involved can collaborate more closely on how to proceed from there. In this way, the partners can decide to act differently, to attempt to improve. It doesn't suggest that they are wrong, bad, or inadequate.

Making Choices

Synergistic coaching attempts to create room for the participants to make choices about changes, adjustments, or new initiatives that will have their deep and personal commitment. Coaching is designed to help those who want to change. They can improve the way they feel about their partners, their business associates, or their significant others. Most importantly, they can change how they feel about themselves and about the relationships they are establishing.

When we choose the coaching option, we need to place some trust in the process. We need to be aware of our tendencies to rely on control, or giving orders, rather than coaching our partners to think for themselves. Again, some striking statistics shed light on the size of this problem. A study by Dr. Jan Halper of 4,000 managers showed that over half of the subjects had the traits of a perfectionist and felt that delegation meant giving up control. Over a fourth felt that associates who showed initiative caused managers to question their self-worth. Slightly less than two thirds were uncomfortable when they allowed others to learn from mistakes. The study members believed they were responsible for results and felt that errors reflected negatively on them. It is clear that old patterns and experiences in life will pull us away from a coaching-style relationship.

When we are tuned in, interested, and willing to help others in a non-manipulative way, we are involved in effective coaching.

Coaching Highs

Synergistic coaching refers to the quality of communications around important matters. Often, these important matters focus on tasks, goals, assignments, progress, new opportunities, and personal development. With coaching, we enable others to grow and learn from the experiences and activities that we share with them. Ultimately, the coaching experience leads to positive action and results that are mutually beneficial to the individuals and to the group.

You don't have to be perfect at working the process. You must simply become "good" at using it—by becoming relatively consistent at it.

Coaching doesn't have to be overly serious. It can be an enjoyable way to help others, without taking control or becoming dependent on one party or the other for answers. At its most basic level, coaching embodies a concept of healthy relationships and communications between members of a group, unit, or team. In today's demanding world, we are often under pressure. Sometimes we are attacked and confronted. We need partners who can create a safe harbor. We see too many people getting hurt by friendly fire. Too often, our associates, friends, and leaders inadvertently shoot us down. Coaching can create a cease fire—and create seamless relationships. Coaches work to promote the talents and potential of the individuals on the team, to motivate people to get excited and enthused about helping the group achieve its purpose.

Literally everyone can become a coach!

360° Coaching

Coaching is not simply a tool for those in authority. It is not exclusively a top-down technique. Rather, it is a process that can be used between team members, and it helps members talk to leaders and leaders talk to members. The coaching process is for anyone who might want to exercise positive influence and help the team succeed. It all starts with communication. When it is done correctly, coaching handles tension without damaging relationships. Coaching goes to important core issues without damaging the bone, organs, or sinew. More aggressive or hostile approaches damage the soft tissue and all of the vital parts of a healthy relationship such as integrity, character, trust, and respect.

The true test of a coach is his or her ability to facilitate others' success in working toward shared goals.

Coaching doesn't necessarily make life easy. However, it does make life respectful, more enjoyable, and much more interesting and hopeful.

This concept is accomplished by helping the partners stay in sync and focused on a common vision without using fear, threats, pessimism, or other negative tactics. These negative approaches can threaten the viability and long-term success of a group. This style of relating helps maintain a strong sense of community—of useful cohesiveness.

In the following chapter, we will broadly describe synergistic coaching in terms of goals, skills, style, function, and values. Our focus will be to provide a full sense of the meaning and application of the coaching process.

Chapter 4
The Goals, Skills, and Outcomes of Synergistic Coaching

The art of putting what you think, feel, or see into words is a deceptively simple skill. The most challenging skill is expressing yourself in an authentic way by effectively converting intentions, thoughts, and feelings into words.

The Coach

Chapter 4
The Goals, Skills, and Outcomes of Synergistic Coaching

The Coaching Goals

Synergistic coaching is designed to tap into people's creative energy and turn on their talents. Synergistic coaching means more than simply getting by, getting along, or getting ahead on your own. The hope is that through constructive dialogue, thinking can be enriched, responses can be expanded, and ingenuity can be ignited. In turn, this should reduce dependency on authority, rules, and formally stated policies.

When two people are involved in the coaching experience, both partners act as leaders, with minimal reliance on power, position, or authority.

"Synergistic Coaching"

The **synergistic** coaching process helps **energize** and uplift participants so they will be more interested and willing to try new ideas and expand their efforts. The goal is to help unleash the motivation within, to do more than simply "go through the motions" of the task or simply punching the time clock. Coaching discourages members of a group from becoming negative, defiant, or rebellious toward their team and its mission. High-performance teams clearly enroll members to pull together in order to help each other, serve the customer better, operate safely, reduce costs, and improve competitive positions. This is important because in the game of life, a coach can't always select his or her favorite starters. Everyone is involved in playing the game, and very often, the coach serves as scorekeeper and helps gauge progress.

To survive, organizations must provide for and respond to the needs of their members, customers, and other stakeholders. Coaching helps people figure out what their needs are and how to respond to them. Coaching is not just for "problem" situations. It helps make the most of positive situations that need to be extended, expanded, and shared with others. This is done by encouraging risk taking and promoting discretionary efforts (above and beyond the call of duty) that will build and move the group to higher levels of effectiveness. There is an important point here. Many people ask us to teach them how to apply coaching to a positive opportunity or situation that is not problem-oriented or a "deficit". We keep saying it doesn't matter. The coach doesn't see a difference; the coach sees each one as a synergistic coaching situation and strives to make it a positive learning, growing experience.

> Everyone is involved in playing the game.

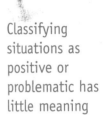

> Classifying situations as positive or problematic has little meaning for a coach.

Successful Failures

All too often, we are unable to capitalize on a situation when we fall short of the mark. Coaching salvages these opportunities. Coaching seeks to learn from the experience and to move away from finger-pointing. If we can create openness by looking at the process more and the intent or motive of people less, each situation (or problem, if you have to call it that) can teach us more. In short, we can have very profitable and successful failures.

> Look at the process more than motive and intent.

Synergistic coaching can be an extremely powerful method to help turn critical and difficult situations around. All too often, struggles and letdowns are handled by attacking and diminishing the self-esteem of others. Too often, relationships are turned into a battlefield with a tragic loss of effectiveness. Coaching helps those who want to become more empowered and encourages members to reach out and achieve new heights—thereby promoting teamwork over individual self-interest. Coaching looks at mistakes, oversights, and problems as learning experiences—like paying tuition. Once a person pays the tuition, he or she then identifies the lesson and plans how to apply it in the future.

One of the major goals of coaching is to create greater trust, while generating less fear.

Synergistic coaching thrives in an environment of trust and mutual respect. In fact, one of the major goals of coaching is to create greater trust, while generating less fear. Coaching also provides more information, less anxiety, and greater clarity and frankness. It enhances one's confidence and self esteem, which are critical for a life of personal fulfillment.

Synergistic coaching is a process that encourages members to move beyond their current levels of effectiveness. This is done through constructive reflection and examining existing comfort levels and current perspectives and mindsets. In order to be the best we can be, we need to use all our resources. Then support is provided as new ideas and energy flow to achieve new levels of knowledge, skill, and ability. The goal of coaching is to help people *reach their true potential.* Coaching promotes continual change, facilitates the success of our partners, and sustains the overall effectiveness of the team. If we are to realize our true potential, we need all that coaching provides.

Coaching builds strengths. It helps neutralize weaknesses, while at the same time encouraging participants to stretch and take intelligent risks. When we are in the coaching process, we are not behaving like kings, where we expect people to respond like robots and to act in a totally compliant manner. However, coaching should help provide a catalyst, define a vision, and generate commitment so that individual members become synchronized with the goals, values, and vision of the entire group.

Good ideas and excellence originate with people, not programs, fads, or the latest technology. People produce goods and services; they save the money and satisfy the customer. Debbie Fields, of Mrs. Fields' Cookies, captured this notion with the corporate logo: "Cookies are our product, but people are our business." How, if we don't build coaching relationships, will we ever find break-through ideas?! We must resist the pressures of time constraints, the fear of openness, disclosure, dialogue, and doubt, in order to help create the right conditions for coaching success.

Great organizations, classrooms, and communities will "spring up" in a coaching field.

Coaching, while not the answer to all problems, does provide a foundation upon which to build for the future.

Stated simply, successful relationships and effective communication make up the foundation, or subplot, for the accomplishments of truly great partnerships.

Coaching Skills

For coaching to be done well, unique skills are required. True coaches know that outstanding results can be achieved only by working with others, not by the coach merely scoring the points. Working effectively with others means that a person must learn to communicate in a way that enhances dignity, respect, and trust. This is true, regardless of what else is transpiring on the playing field or the routine pressures that are bearing down on the partners.

Coaches try to maximize collaboration and participation to ensure adult-to-adult communications.

The synergistic coaching process does not rely on prescribed solutions or directives, but rather on mutual understanding, fact finding, careful, thorough reflection, creative action planning, and compassionate follow-up.

The coaching process is designed to promote good will, optimism, open communications, and commitment to succeed—both on an individual and team level.

Coaching depends heavily on our ability to accept challenges and new data, not be defensive, and keep an open mind.

When you are coaching, ask yourself:

- *What can I learn from the other person?*

- *Am I prepared to learn?*

- *Am I willing to suspend criticism, let go of some control, and be more vulnerable and open to others?*

Coaching encompasses our ability to see new things in new ways and to accept change and shifts in paradigms.

Coaching partners are dedicated to understanding, consideration, trust, discovery, personal reflection, change, and action. As the coach deals with obstacles as learning opportunities, members are able to "positively" serve each other in their mutual effort or mission.

Coaching builds on and reinforces relationships with others. The coaching process attempts to balance individual needs with the needs of the task and the team. Effective coaches are able to successfully merge the interests of the group with those of the individual players. Coaches strive to build win/win relationships so that everyone has a chance to gain and feel positive about their function within the group. Ultimately the coach becomes a mere reflection of the team or partnership.

Coaching exchanges control for long-term commitment, fierce loyalty, and alignment.

Coaching requires practice, work, and conscious choices to put into play the skills, knowledge, and abilities that will be addressed in the ensuing chapters. The coaching skills, as well as the coaching style, call for reductions in authoritarian tactics, coercion, and intimidation, which produce fear and dependency and do not build and develop human potential. Coaching does not depend on position, power, or authority to influence participants to act appropriately and effectively. It exchanges control for long-term commitment, fierce loyalty, and alignment. Even so, let's not minimize the fact that the coaching process exists to achieve results and facilitate team achievements. In a synergistic partnership, individuals do well in order to help achieve a successful end result for the group as a whole.

Fundamentally, the coaching process must respect and be a steward for the needs of all stakeholders of the group: doers, peers, owners, customers, students, family members, or friends. Each team member's ability to balance these needs and then improve, depends on productive dialogue, two-way interaction, and effective listening. It also encompasses personal reflection, introspection, and creativity.

Facilitating Honorably

Again, incorporating all of these elements does not absolutely insure success. Sometimes, even with flawless use of coaching skills, some members are determined to support their own myopic, short-sighted self inter-est, rather than their long-term interests and the overall needs of the group. The coaching process is focused on

A coach, no mater how effective, cannot *force* a team member to participate in the coaching process.

nurturing individuals into increasingly stronger players, no matter how advanced the player is. If a participant will shed the shackles of selfishness and commit to advancing the effectiveness of the group, then the synergistic coaching process can work its magic.

Those who have learned to be effective coaches realize that change and development cannot be forced. They realize that there is no quick fix and that they cannot work miracles. They cannot take ownership for the actions, attitudes, or beliefs of others. As facilitators, or catalysts, for growth and change, they provide an additional source of feedback about situations and events that individuals encounter in life.

Coaches must learn not to take things personally and go ballistic when they do not see the desired progress taking place.

Instead, coaches must allow agency for their partner and coach "from their own perspective." They must understand that coaching is a 50/50 collaboration. One partner cannot have a hidden agenda. He or she cannot attempt to upstage or try to look better than the other person.

Coaching is a 50/50 collaboration.

As a coach, a person must become somewhat dispassionate, less emotional, and must follow the coaching road map in order to achieve understanding. Synergy and cooperation must occur in a non-manipulative way. More openness can be achieved if the coaching dialogue takes place non-aggressively, so the recipient does not feel attacked and with a need to defend.

Trust the coaching road map.

It is no secret that too many organizations are built upon a sandy foundation of authority, controls, procedures, and bureaucracy. However, successful relationships cannot be built using such traditional methods. This is why coaching is so important. Instead of these oppressive elements, more positive and constructive processes must be adopted. Excessive rules, regulations, and procedures tend to be restrictive—they do not empower, excite, or motivate. Excessive controls will result in conformity, rather than substance. Rules and regulations need to be in balance—too much or too little is devastating to your vitality, vigor, and health. For some, synergistic coaching will appear to be going against the traditional, authoritative grain. In fact, it will feel a little different for both parties. It is just not a regular part of the way society and civilizations operate yet. But it

Coaching requires a little courage and risk-taking.

is the path we must follow in the future if society is to progress. It requires a little courage and risk-taking to get the coaching pattern going, but the effort is well worth it!

Teachers, leaders, and parents often over-focus on problems in relationships. Excess worry leads them to become reactionary in dealing with others. Coaching creates a new framework—a different way of responding to challenges. Our society needs consensus, not force. Consensus and openness bring enthusiasm and vibrancy to relationships.

Fundamentally, coaching is a basic view of human behavior that is expressed in supportive interaction.

It requires that we become genuinely interested in

 others. Otherwise, we may spend hours with a mirror in our hand, admiring our own greatness and losing ourselves in selfishness and self-absorption. When the mirror is turned around, the team members look at themselves and reflect, then explore not only their own potential, but the synergism they can create with their partners.

Exceptional partnerships call for both members to think and act like a coach.

Without question, commitment and a willingness to devote time and energy are needed to learn the nuances of coaching. It is not an either-or proposition. If people choose to structure their relationships around the coaching model, they must reach out and learn what others want, how they feel, how they view their world—and then be willing to speak up when opportunities and teaching situations emerge. By incorporating coaching as the routine mode of operation, the partners build up a "JOINT" bank account of trust and respect that either person can share and draw on. When legitimate emergencies or crises arise, either member can lead a coaching discussion without creating hostility and negative emotional baggage.

The skilled coach can push constructive thoughts past their lips, even though they may be feeling upset, frustrated, or ready to lash out. Keep in mind that coaching is not a benign, permissive strategy in which one imposes questionable motives or will upon others. Coaching does not mean lowering standards or accepting mediocrity. Healthy relationships require understanding, reciprocity, flexibility, and a willingness to contribute. In short, synergistic coaching seeks an environment of cooperation and creativity.

Deutch's Law

Dr. Robert Deutch, a noted sociologist, presented a law of human relationships which has been appropriately labeled "Deutch's Law." In short, this law states that, "the more we act in certain ways, the more others around us act in the very same ways." Others have labeled this the "Law of Reciprocity," simply because behaving in an understanding, collaborative way creates an environment for the partner to respond in the very same way. Trusting, respectful behavior breeds a trusting, respectful response. This law of reciprocity is the flip side to the Golden Rule— that is, do unto others as they would have you do unto them.

There are actually two parts to this idea. The first is the "ripple effect," and the second is the "restoration effect." When a coach sends out positive ripples of understanding, the receiver responds to the original sender with the same type of behavior, the restoration effect. It becomes an upward spiraling process.

People experience increased self-esteem, and the group as a whole can increase its effectiveness and productivity as the process expands to others.

Benevolent Openness

This principle is the key ingredient that allows the coaching process to succeed.

Closely akin to Deutch's Law, and actually the premise for it, is the principle that we call "benevolent openness." It reflects the notion that, in our primary and secondary relationships, we should be "benevolently open" to the opportunities and the struggles others are having. In other words, we should be observant, notice, and look for learning opportunities. However, we must refrain from being controlling and inflexible. When the waters are calm in relationships, this is quite easy to accomplish. The real test, of course, is when a person seems "out of line" and we are tempted by a traditional harsh response, or when our partners become resistant and will not explore opportunities that may be obscure to them.

We all short-circuit at times.

In essence, this principle provides for *human error*. We all short-circuit at times, especially when the group system is traumatized or when individuals are trying to deal with stress in their lives. Yet, this is the very time that the coaching model allows the parties to take the "high road" in the way they respond to each other.

Still, each party cannot expect to get everything he or she wants. It requires effort to achieve understanding, respect, and communication—to discover the synergistic possibilities. The coaching process simply invites each party to work harder at explaining more, while criticizing less. Its aim is relationship therapy—

not relationship surgery—and the working through of differences to achieve mutual agreements. We must risk more by constructively working things out, rather than ignore, cover up, attack, gossip, or verbally abuse others.

Each party cannot expect to get everything he or she wants.

The "Third" Partner

The coaching process tries to make not only both parties happy and more effective, but all "three" parties happier and more effective. What we mean is that in coaching, a third party is always involved. The third party could be the class, the family, the team, the business, the customer, or the community. Both coaching parties must have a strong sensitivity to, and clear vision, of the needs of the invisible third party. The interest of the third party frequently is not as well represented in the discussion; but it is nevertheless greatly affected by our choices, actions, and attitudes. The coaching process seeks to merge the needs, views, and diversity of all three parties into a collaborative, shared vision for the entire organization.

Coaching Applications

When coaching happens in a very casual way, it almost becomes a routine way of relating.

The applications of the coaching process are varied. It can apply to a broad range of relationship situations. It can be used to help teach and train, to inspire, to motivate, and to enhance performance. Coaching is a useful way to reward and reinforce, to recognize and affirm, to provide positive feedback by showing appreciation, and to work through conflicts and differences. A coach can also serve as a mentor, empowering others to pursue new opportunities and creative directions, thereby fulfilling their life goals and hopes.

We have invited hundreds of individuals to describe when and how they would utilize coaching skills and principles. The diagram on the following page captures some of the key responses we have received.

Because the coaching umbrella covers a wide range of activities, it is possible to constantly influence and build meaningful relationships. In this sense, coaching should not, as a rule, be a formal process.

The Coaching Umbrella

◆ Adapting to change

◆ Peer to peer discussions

◆ Developing creative ideas together

◆ Safety discussions

◆ Reinforcing successes and building strengths

◆ Communicating "up" to leaders

◆ Planning career paths

◆ Responding to problems and concerns

◆ When someone seeks your input

◆ Pursuing new oppotrunities

◆ Helping others adjust to new requirements

◆ Performance planning

◆ Developing new talents

◆ Developing expectations with new members

◆ Working through conflict and resistance

◆ Adjusting to new assignments

◆ Taking some reasonable risks

◆ Solving production and quality problems

◆ Helping groups or teams work through issues

◆ Using difficult situations to learn for the future

◆ Periodic progress reviews

◆ Responding to grievances

◆ Building alliances with other teams or departments

◆ Enhancing even good relationships

**Coaching can also be a formal activity,
established on a regular basis.**

For example, you might choose one day each month
to literally sit down and discuss previous events, as
well as upcoming activities and strategies. One person
who has found value using the coaching process in a
formal way is a vice president of a large Canadian
company. As she explained it, "I can't run the business
without my weekly **fireside chat**, where we can cover
tasks, processes, and relationship objectives." Whether
formal or informal, however, it should contain non-
threatening dialogue, build on mutual learning, and
create a win/win outcome, rather than become a
contest in which one party proves the
other wrong.

I can't run the business without my weekly "fireside chat."

Vertical vs. Lateral Relationships

In observing truly functional family relationships—
parent to child, or partner to partner—we see members treating each other as equals, with respect and
trust. In less-functional relationships, they treat
others in a condescending manner. This "one-up"
relationship is called a VERTICAL RELATIONSHIP.
Vertical relationships are counter-productive. They
sabotage themselves, and ultimately the person in the
"one-down" position rebels and aborts the relationship.

These unhealthy vertical relationships are found too
often in society. While it may initially appear that
they can continue on ad infinitum, without impairing

the association, they cannot. An exploitive, manipulative relationship ultimately cripples the foundation of support and trust that otherwise anchors the organization. Most formal organizations create relationships in a rigid, vertical "chain of command." While this looks logical on paper, it does not help teams achieve high-performance, and extraordinary results. It may "seem" orderly to manage relationships "top down," but order is a shallow asset. Associates at work or at home will be more focused if they work in tandem with you.

The key to synergistic coaching, then, is to cause individuals to self-examine their motives and behavioral patterns with their "significant others," and to then create an environment that will encourage and foster balanced or lateral relationships. Less control and manipulation create the opportunity for more flexibility and creativity.

Proper coaching involves exploring more, while attempting to correct and change less—especially in a forced way.

As we have previously stated, in some ways, life resembles the world of athletics. In sports, there are always opportunities to call "time out" and to engage in scheduled "half-time" discussions. Effective use of time-outs and half-time adjustments often means the difference between success and failure. The same is true with life. Most relationships and individuals will be more productive if people spend some time discussing progress, expectations, hopes, and needs, as well as problems and opportunities. The goal is for these quality interactions to occur before we are "behind in the game," before people become emotional, desperate, or explosive.

Talk, Listen, and Act

Many organizations have institutionalized the coaching process. One of our clients refers to this as TLA, or "talk, listen, and act." These formal coaching opportunities show a strong commitment to coaching. Even so, simply institutionalizing it is not going to guarantee quality coaching results unless the skills, values, and willingness to invest in the work are clearly voluntary. Still, the formal scheduled time-out session, or discussion, can be seen as a miniature quality circle, or continuous improvement team.

The Subject Matter

Coaching discussions can focus on new assignments and responsibilities, as well as obstacles and challenges that may be of concern to either party. You might review new ideas, breakthroughs, and opportunities that could be pursued. Coaches can also focus on self-development activities, progress, or opportunities for training and individual development plans. The discussion could include a review of expectations for new or changing roles and responsibilities. The coaching dialogue could also focus on relationships and interactions with co-workers, management, customers, suppliers, and so forth.

Most people prefer some regular time-out discussion to check on understandings and agreements, and to ensure alignment.

One of our coaching studies showed that most people prefer some regular time-out discussion to check on understandings and agreements, and to ensure alignment. We have found that team members have a stronger appetite to receive coaching, feedback, and communication than many of us have the strength to give. We must remember, however, that event coaching or "interval coaching" should not be used to

replace other processes and practices such as
"open door policies," all-employee meetings,
and various team-building initiatives. It
should not remove the responsibility for on-
the-spot coaching. When we use a "reactive
coaching" response to urgent situations and
problems, we lose significant learning opportunities and reduce our effectiveness. "Proactive"
coaching is simply looking forward, coaching ahead,
and anticipating deeply important issues that may
affect your partnerships.

A coach should not measure the quality of the coaching by the number of required or formally scheduled
coaching sessions. The true test of quality is the
strength of the coach's commitment to interaction
and dialogue—as well as the coach's style and genuine interest in the other person. The formal interval
session is more or less a capstone of the coaching
process. It makes a significant statement, but not
nearly as much as spontaneous acts or regular, day-
to-day interactions.

Coaching Outcomes

Earlier in this chapter, we alluded to the fact that
coaching has a price. Dues must be paid in order to
form effective relationships and productive dialogues.
Coaching is not initially implemented without some
pain and discomfort. But the benefits are significant
for those who make the journey both for themselves,
and for the organization as a whole—not the least of
which is the special knowledge that people share
when the coaching spirit is present. People seem to
open up more, defend less, disclose their true feelings,
and focus on more creative solutions, while showing
greater resolve to explore new ideas. In one of our
more recent studies, coaches reported high commit-

ment levels, enthusiasm, and motivation among team members.

The Coaching Trend

We have found that people simply like the coaching process. They enjoy participating, both as the coach and as the partner.

At times we tend to focus the coaching on end results, or the bottom line. While this is important, most people say they use the coaching process for themselves, as well.

It helps them feel better about the collaboration, and dealing positively with the opportunities and challenges that arise enhances their self-esteem. They don't feel badly because there is no attack and no motive for resentful feelings or revenge.

One of our clients reported that using the coaching process has become a profound "self-talk approach" when working through specific situations. This client shared with us a serious life challenge and how the coaching model was used to successfully work through it. Her spouse was seriously disabled by an unfortunate accident. This accident required major life-style changes, changes in behavior and in thought patterns and perceptions based on coping with a very different life and trying to find a new comfort zone. The coaching process helped her stay focused and upbeat. Coaching helped her create ideas and responses to new and difficult problems in her life.

Certainly coaching helps any partnership, or group, achieve more and become more proficient. This is accomplished when partners use fewer resources, or use them more effectively. We have also observed many organizations that have benefited from coaching in terms of safety performance, personal development, and individual character development. For example, in one major Fortune 500 company we worked with, the coaching process became one of several key variables that lead to a 23% improvement in safety performance. This was accomplished over a one-year time period by consciously using the coaching process, as well as other very important supporting interventions, on a regular basis. In a large east coast refinery, coaching helped people become more productive and open to change. Over a two-year period, this organization started making a profit after five years of straight losses. It has also been used to build consensus and unity around organization values, norms, and principles. Others have seen the coaching process enhance creativity and learning.

We have found that individuals who engage in coaching are able to create more healthy and well-rounded relationships. Over the past decade, many authors, including the late Edwards Deming, have written about the benefits of driving fear out of an organization. Coaching is an ideal mechanism to accomplish this and to create a positive work climate. Reducing stress and anxiety, as well as promoting healthy and positive attitudes toward change, enhance the long-term health and well-being of an organization. Team members will gradually acquire a sense of stewardship for their responsibilities and become more self-directed. This growth allows the group to re-deploy critical management and leadership resources. People will use each other as a sounding board for problems and decisions and not a parking lot where they try to off-load problems onto each other.

Both parties must inquire and discover, as well as advocate and assert.

These results illustrate the power of the coaching process, and similar results are attainable if the engaging parties are willing to participate in coaching.

Even though coaching can bring these achievements, in some organizations, people still choose to shape their relationships in a very traditional fashion.

Too many people look at relationships as a commodity and feel that people can simply be treated like any other piece of equipment.

Herein lies both the mystery and the opportunity of coaching! Human behavior is complex, and it is not always easy making human processes operate the way we would like. Even so, the real gains in creating high-quality communications are well worth the effort.

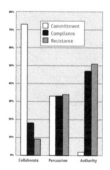

Precise measurement is difficult.

We have found that it is very difficult to measure caring, creativity, loyalty, concentration, dedication, commitment, and motivation. The problem is that all too often, we become too focused on spending a lot of energy trying to measure these qualities in statistical ways or with accounting tools. Measuring and controlling the variables that affect how much people choose to contribute will always be difficult. That is the beauty of it. Those who trust the process will gain, while others sit around debating how to measure the details.

Relationships are everything, and people who have learned to trust this process find that coaching truly is common sense, and that all we are attempting to do is move it to our personal and organization's frontal lobe. Again, we must remember that to a certain degree coaching is simply common sense. Even though coaching is common sense, in far too many relationships, coaching is not common practice. We need to constantly remind ourselves that in any organized team endeavor, it is the players who produce results and make the operation a daily success.

Coaching is the instrument through which we can invest in our players.

We must operate from our belief systems and from deep values that assure us that, in the long run, coaching is absolutely the best policy.

In our workshops, we are constantly bombarded with questions and requests. One person, for example, wanted to become better at learning coaching tools and techniques. Unfortunately, when some people say they are looking for "tools," what they mean is that they are looking for "weapons!" They fail to see that they, themselves, accompanied by their values and communicative abilities, are the tools. They don't need more manipulation, power, or control. To the contrary, they simply need patience in learning specific coaching skills that will help them clarify and re-focus their energies. Many times, we have seen situations where the coach's impatience and desire for quick results ran head-on into another person's resistance to control, stubbornness, and blind spots.

Everyone seems to be looking for the "quick fix."

Coaching and Empowerment

EMPOWERMENT means accepting responsibility for creating the type of environment we want. Empowerment embodies the act of standing on our own ground, discovering our own voice, making our own choices—regardless of the level of power and privilege we hold. It stems from our choice, from our mind-set that guides and reminds us that we have within ourselves the authority to act and to speak and to serve those around us. We don't need to be coronated as coaches. We don't need a job title that identifies us as a coach. We simply need to realize that if the individual and teams are to be sharp and on the growth path, we must have a sense of empowerment. We must accept the responsibility to shape and influence the direction of our relationships.

> ## We must decide to be "contributors" to the relationship, and not simply be "along for the ride."

We must take some risks by speaking up gracefully and becoming a partner in growth. We do not need permission to feel or to take what matters to us into our own hands.

Empowerment is simply the ability to follow or act upon one's vision.

Becoming empowered is a very vogue and powerful process, for both individuals and for organizations. From our experience, the coaching dialogue facilitates empowerment as a means of defining purpose for ourselves and our key relationships. In essence, we empower ourselves to choose and then talk about the type of environment and communications we want to create—both for ourselves and for our organization. Without waiting for the top leaders (CEO, principal, owner, president, etc.) to "declare their vision," we commit ourselves emotionally to building productive partnerships. With this commitment, we relegate to second place our need to "build our personal career," win every argument, dictate decisions, and ignore the input and contributions of others.

Empowerment DOESN'T mean that you make decisions on your own.

Empowerment, from the coaching perspective, is the way to create less dependency, helplessness, or indifference. With coaching, we choose to join with others, to intervene in a consensual, synergistic way. The need for higher levels of involvement from and communication between individuals is paramount. We like the description of empowerment offered by Daryl R. Conner in his book *Managing at the Speed of Change.* To paraphrase: The antithesis of empowerment is victimization. Partners help you avoid the pitfalls of victim mentality. You are empowered when you are perceived as a valued resource. You are empowered when you constructively influence others' decisions.

From our experience, it is not a matter of IF the coaching process will enter organizations that really want to succeed, but WHEN! After numerous coaching projects with other organizations around the world, it has become clear to us that incorporating INVOLVEMENT, EMPOWERMENT, CREATIVITY, and TEAMWORK will ultimately become the competitive advantage.

We have discovered that the members of organizations in some cultures do not seem to have an abundance of sensitivity toward the long-term health of their organizations. Additionally, the entrepreneurial instinct doesn't appear as strong as it could be. To the contrary, the social-economic "safety net" protects employees better and often creates an unhealthy entitlement mentality and dependence on authorities to take responsibility for problems and new opportunities. Interestingly, in some prosperous countries, there have been few recessions and downsizing in the past few decades. This historical fact almost breeds a bit of a self-centered motive for joining an organization. In some cases, laws make it more difficult to down-size, or re-deploy people, in order to achieve success.

Some people see work as a right and the organization as a welfare agency.

While the "authoritarian modus operandi" is prevalent in many societies, emphasizing the need for individuals to "not question authority," this unhealthy attitude breeds the "why worry about our team" attitude.

Today's markets are clearly the targets of global competition, and we must face the harsh reality that some organizations are out of shape, bureaucratic, over-staffed, and have some "dead wood." These organizations may require major structural adjustments before the coaching process has a very good chance of working. General Electric realized this a few years ago and has taken major steps to get in shape and really used its "work out" meetings as a coaching vehicle.

Need Fulfillment

If we care about our organization's long-term viability, and if we want to help our associates "fulfill their needs," as Abraham Maslow taught in his much heralded Hierarchy of Needs paradigm, then we must adopt the mindset unveiled in  synergistic coaching. As the pressure for results builds, we must have committed associates with a sure knowledge that their needs are a strategic priority. As one of our clients, Charlie, with a Fortune 20 company said, "I want a signal that this is a place where I want to 'stake down' my tent." Charlie's statement applies to businesses as well as to government, classrooms, charity organizations, and families.

 We expect that in the future, we will see leaner organizations, with less lead time to achieve their objectives and with greater pressure to reduce costs while increasing productivity. At the same time, these organizations will begin to enhance quality and improve their position in the marketplace.

These pressures do not make it easy for coaches to maintain a balance between task needs and people needs. At times, the owners and investors, as well as some of the "bean counters," are only concerned with short-term costs and bottom-line profitability. At the same time, customers expect more quality, value, and service. They are very impatient and quick to "shop around" to find better values. In addition, talented members of organizations desire better treatment and recognition, as well as an opportunity to share in the gains realized through their services. They are interested in value, recognition, opportunities, and quality relationships.

It is also true that some members are too needy, greedy, self-centered, fearful, and unwilling to embrace change and improvement. They may evolve into long-term coaching projects, requiring a lot of patience. As coaches, you will need to find the right role for them to fit into to ensure their ultimate success.

As you become increasingly successful, you may discover that you LIVE TO WORK, and not simply WORK TO LIVE. People who really contribute do not want to be manipulated or ignored.

People want to become involved and need to be "coached" rather than "controlled."

If people don't find fulfillment, they will let their feet do the walking and will shop for a place that allows them to feel like an integral part of the greater whole. As one of our clients describes this phenomenon, we must adopt the "long view." We must look beyond the horizon, not only in terms of technology and investment, but also in terms of a highly valued work environment.

Adopt the "long view."

Patience

With patience and time, the coaching process can become a vital part of your daily thoughts and actions. Coaching is a paradigm shift for many—but once people begin to think and act like coaches, the coaching processes becomes internalized. Ultimately, coaching skills will enhance their identity and be woven into the fabric of their very character. Then, without compulsory action, their own level of coaching will be elevated. They will begin to make room for the needs of others and become much greater contributors to their relationships.

Coaching is a paradigm shift for many—but once people begin to think, talk, and act like coaches, the "coaching process" becomes a basic part of us.

Perhaps this ultimate "life change" can best be delineated by two very opposing operational definitions of love. The first is a very selfish definition, which states that, "WE LOVE OR ADMIRE OR CARE ABOUT ONLY THOSE WHO SATISFY OUR NEEDS." The opposite view, which is an outcropping of the synergistic coaching philosophy, states that, "WE SATISFY THE NEEDS OF THOSE WE LOVE OR ADMIRE OR CARE ABOUT—BOTH FOR THEIR PERSONAL BENEFIT, AS WELL AS FOR THE GOOD OF THE ENTIRE GROUP."

The first of these is a very "self-centered" orientation toward relationships. The partner, the group, or the organization exists only to meet the personal needs of the person. The second, however, demonstrates an "other-oriented" philosophy. This focus, born of selflessness, will ultimately benefit not only the individual experiencing it, but it will ripple out into the organization.

In conclusion, the coaching process will ultimately impact not only our accomplishments, but more importantly, our basic feelings and beliefs. We believe that this internalization of support and concern for others, and ultimately for the organization, elevates thoughts and behaviors, the ramifications of which can and will impact all of society.

"Other-oriented" philosophy

Chapter 5
The Coaching Model—
An Overview

The effective leader coach has the ability to be firm and fair, to push at the right time and yet be flexible at the appropriate moment. These themes are embedded in our data and reinforce the "support-initiate" concept in coaching.

The Coach

Chapter 5
The Coaching Model—
An Overview

Purpose and Direction

This chapter provides a broad overview of the coaching process and our eight-step coaching model. A general working framework of this model will give the reader a better understanding of the whole. In subsequent chapters, we will progress deeply into the various elements of the coaching model. Like flying in an airplane at an altitude of 40,000 feet, this chapter is intended to provide the reader with a "lay of the land." In the chapters that follow, we will dive down and explore detailed features of the coaching terrain.

The coaching model is not a prescription or a "cook book" of techniques.

By way of introduction, the coaching model is not a prescription or a "cook book" of techniques. It looks fairly simple and easy to apply, but it is not simplistic. The model is a mirror image of what we see and hear happening as people establish quality interactions with others. Enormous flexibility is required by the vast array of situations and personalities that shape these elements into an effective road map.

Coaching also has form and structure, but it also requires flexibility and judgment.

We have often likened the coaching model to a musical keyboard. Many who operate this keyboard may compose the music extemporaneously. Others may want to plan and write the music down before they even approach the keyboard. The process may even involve both approaches: there may be some initial planning combined with a lot of spontaneity as the rhythm and tone evolve and adjustments are made. Like music, there is room for guidelines and creativity.

Coaching Model

The Eight Steps of the Coaching Model are placed in a circle to illustrate the continual, ongoing nature of the coaching process. This series is not intended to imply a rigid, set order in which the steps are played out in the dialogue, or relationship. In other words, it is not necessary to mechanically begin with Step One. Any of these steps can be a starting point, depending on where two people are in a relationship or life cycle of a particular topic or issue. For example, if there has been ongoing dialogue or a series of meetings, a person might start with some initial support and review progress in Step Four (The Plan) or Step Five (The Commitment). It would be just as logical to begin with Step Seven or Eight, to engage the other person in a discussion of the outcomes and then celebrate success thus far.

The starting point is a "floating point." Even though this is so, Step One is the core element; without it, a meaningful collaborative coaching dialogue cannot unfold.

The larger the support "joint bank account" a partnership has, the better. If a relationship has a low bank account of support, members may need to invest additional effort in this step before moving into substantive issues or topics. In fact, entire discussions could be built around creating rapport and helping build trust and openness in the relationship.

Each step is a different color. The warm yellows are used to send a message of acceptance. The red shades indicate some tension, a need to stop or slow down, and to then proceed at a slower pace. The discussion could heat up, which is okay, as long as the topic doesn't boil over and explode. The "red" tension can be good or bad depending on how you work with it.

The blue represents moving forward into the future. It portrays "blue sky," or thinking that the "sky is the limit."

In the blue zone, people talk about possibilities for the future, and then create agreements, select plans, and reach decisions. Purple, the unique color, is in need of special consideration. Many people like purple, while some detest it. It can have a positive or negative connotation. A person must read the situation, then determine how best to work with this step.

Step One, after all, is the *center* of the coaching process; support is the element that links the entire model together into one whole. We can have many levels of relationships with people, but if support is not at the core, if the dues are not paid, we will simply not have a coaching-oriented partnership. From the data we have collected over the years, there is just no way around this fact. Positive intentions need to exist and we need to remain in touch with this step by our words and actions. This one step touches all of the other steps in the model and the path from one step to another is usually through the center step. Even when coaching mistakes are made, Step One is the best remedy. Support is what we fall back on when things get out of hand. Thus, it deserves this special position in our model. It is reported that Abraham Maslow said it takes nine positive or supportive comments to make up for one negative or scolding type of remark.

Nine positive comments are needed to offset one negative.

The word "step" is used in identifying the individual elements of the coaching model and indicates that IN A GENERAL SENSE, THERE IS A BUILDING PROCESS. Each step is preceded by a step that contributes to the adjoining step. For example, while it is possible for a person to help another create a

In a general sense, there is a building process in the coaching dialogue.

plan (Step Four) without discovering its impact (Step Three), it is more difficult in most cases to do so. The plan will be an easier part of the coaching dialogue if both parties have a healthy understanding and awareness of other viewpoints (Step 3). This *empathic response* takes place when a person is able to step back and discover the blind spots, or the possible incompleteness in the way he or she has been thinking. If a person carefully examines the strengths and weaknesses of the current strategy in a non-personal way, the resulting greater "felt need" or constructive tension will help in designing alternative approaches for the future. The steps in our model then convey a **general** building process. When a person "hits a snag" with his or her partner, steps can be retraced to find whether a particular earlier step may need additional attention in order to achieve a rich dialogue.

One picture certainly doesn't capture reality. The model does not clearly identify the importance—or the time and effort—that typically goes into each step.

For example, Step Five, commitment, is usually not a time-intensive step. Even so, it is extremely critical to the overall success of the coaching process. Furthermore, we have found numerous communication behaviors and skills that make for an effective coaching discussion. However, all of these behaviors are not fully captured in the eight-step model.

In some cases, the identified steps contain a double meaning. For example, in Step Two, an agenda that both parties are comfortable with is needed, yet it must also incorporate the more global vision the parties are striving to achieve. Incorporating and blending both of these ideas into one central point, makes this step more time intensive. It takes time and effort to ensure a common topic and a well-defined guiding direction for the dialogue. Until the guiding direction is established, the coaching process needs to "camp out" on this step and spend some quality time in developing the overall purpose or vision that stands behind the "presenting" topic.

For those of us who are not naturally gifted or talented coaches, the model is a solid framework or template that can prompt us to correctly complete the "preflight check" before we become airborne in the discussion. If a person experiences communication or relationship "vertigo," the coaching model becomes the radar screen and the orienting mechanism. 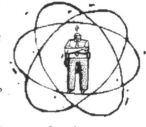 This model provides a straight-forward way in which to have open and constructive interaction and build strong, inclusive relationships rather than a vast array of psycho-sociological theories. The model is a guide to enhance knowledge, build friendships, create understanding, and share wisdom.

The coaching model is not designed to impose a rigid structure. It gives us a soft structure that is aligned with partnership values and principles.

Many of us think in "linear" terms. The coaching model allows us to **begin** thinking about effective dialogue in a sequential way. Some people think of the coaching model as a wiring diagram that hooks up the voltage of synergy and consensus. This, in turn, enables us to discover the art and flexibility that is available to us once we learn how to maneuver and build skills and awareness. Each coaching situation is unique and may not include all eight steps. Instead, we can explore which steps are pertinent. Appropriateness and relevance are the keys with the model as a guide. Coaching is not necessarily segmental despite the appearance of the model.

Be a bit provisional and patient as you work through each step of the process.

The model is a way to achieve constructive openness. It is not designed to be a reprimand, lecture, verbal spanking, or to be parental or authoritative. It is, however, designed to level the dialogue playing field. The coaching model helps you put things in perspective so that mole hills are not turned into mountains.

Through careful and thoughtful application of the coaching model—it becomes something to "practice," not just advocate; then we can achieve a unique relationship that will help both parties learn to make choices that will facilitate the communication. The coaching parties simply need to keep in mind that coaching is designed to help, rather than to "hurt." Through its use, we learn to inquire and learn before we advocate our views and positions. We must appreciate that understanding each others, expectations and perceptions is the key to human compatibility and happiness.

At this time, we would like to scan over the model. In subsequent chapters, we will put a microscope on the steps and get to know them up close and personal.

Step One: Be Supportive

Before embarking along the "coaching path," we must ensure that the parties involved are not on the "war path."

This step occupies the unique "center place" in the coaching model. In terms of a coaching road map, Step One is equivalent to "main street." Open discussion and dialogue do not provide license for a personal "get even" or "pay back" experience. To the contrary, the conversation must be non-adversarial and non-punitive. People must leave their "ego needs" and "defensive barriers" at the doorway before they enter the coaching dialogue. You must make it clear that you mean no harm, that your partner is not a bad person, and that the topic or subject is not personal.

The coaching discussion should promote trust, mutual respect, and total honesty. Compassion and mutual understanding likewise have a place in the coaching process—and in all organizations, businesses, schools, communities, and families. In a remarkable way, support is like the atmosphere of "air." We don't actually see it, but we definitely breathe it in. It is like the outer shell of the environment, and it permeates everything we do. It is also like the jelly roll we sometimes eat for breakfast. We like to taste a little jelly with each bite of the roll.

A person may need to address past baggage and emotions early on, and then determine how to handle them before moving into the topics at hand. This first step not only represents what is said in a supportive way, but also represents each of the unspoken and fine filaments of meaning that are exchanged through eye contact, tone, seating arrangements, location of the discussion, etc.

For some, it is shocking to engage in open and honest dialogue.

For this reason, a coach must prepare in advance by having a feel for the needs, attitudes, and reactions of others. That coach must also determine the best ways to support others as he or she delves into the issues at hand. Learning to support others does not mean artificially sugar coating the topic, trying to smooth it over, or covering up key points.

Jenny, a manager at one of our workshops, expressed her perception this way: "It feels like I am trying too hard to be nice when I'm coaching." Support should not replace honesty, fairness, and objectivity. Rather, it is an attempt to keep the topic and the discussion in perspective. It requires patience, and one cannot fill the void of support with just one meeting. It is good to be nice, but the key is to be clear about the discussion and give honest support.

Supportive coaches are sensitive to the needs and feelings of others.

They should not be overly sensitive to the first impressions others have of them. Clear and open communication may at first appear aggressive if you don't work in ample support. Coaching is an opportunity to build constructive bridges with others. When coaching, be aware of the type of support others need and then not be afraid to express it. Coaches should explain what must happen in order to remain productively engaged. Bottom line, the spirit of this first step is trust, mutual respect, and a sincere desire to collaborate.

Step Two: Define The Topic and Needs

T.S. Eliot said, "We shall never cease discovery."

This step moves from the yellow warmth of supportiveness to an intense red. While we are not suggesting that one must be aggressive and abrupt with the topic and needs, it is important to gain clarity, even at the risk of touching on some tender and sensitive issues. The key to Step Two is to discover the truth and share information so that the facts can be revealed. This helps achieve a mutual clarity. It is also critical to be "lined up" on the same topic, and to gain an agreement on the agenda that doesn't overload the participants or the time needed to sort things out.

At times the topic may be shocking, and there may be feelings of occasional disbelief and denial surfacing in the form of benign excuses and venting. This becomes a problem only if the parties feel the need to refute and debate the feelings or excuses.

The best approach with Step Two is to work from the general to the specific—to draw it out before you draw it for them—to inquire before you advocate a position.

Step Two requires a disclosure of impressions, thoughts, and perspectives. It also requires deep and attentive listening.

If you don't create fear around the topic, you can obtain valuable information and awareness that will add to the learning process. Try to drive around the issue before trying to "drive into" it. This approach will lead to a more complete understanding of the situation. There are always multiple sides to any issue, and a wise coach gently glances at the data from various points of view. In past studies, we have learned that people usually have a pretty good grasp of reality—if they can simply facilitate the discussion, rather than assuming the role of the prosecutor, or interrogator.

If the coach is patient, the truth will ultimately manifest itself.

Getting a handle on the topic is only part of the process outlined in Step Two. The other part deals with the overall need and the deeper underlying principle. The needs are from three perspectives: Party A, Party B, and the group as a whole, Party C. The goal is to merge the needs and locate the common ground.

In most organizations, there is a compelling need or reason why the parties are together. Without some clarity of purpose and direction, it is obvious that the other coaching steps will be merely "token and superficial" at best. For example, in a work group, the compelling need may be to produce the best quality product on the market, and to do so at the lowest price. Thus, the questions are the following: "Are we currently building on what is working?" "Are we eliminating things that don't work?" "Where are we going?" "Where do we want to be in the future?" Individuals have good intentions at heart. They sometimes lack the feedback or perspective from others to help determine whether they are effectively and rapidly moving in the desired direction.

Step Two requires exploring, discovering, and being open, rather than "certainty."

We need to be somewhat provisional and vulnerable to the fact that we rarely have the complete truth. "Certainty" on our part will help drive and fuel resistance and defensiveness. Thus, we should ask good questions, while actively and effectively listening to others. The spirit of this step is one of inquiry and learning. We can't be afraid to label, call out, and name our own biases.

Step Two doesn't suggest that we must agree with everything the other person is saying. Rather, it suggests that it IS important to listen to what others have to say. We should then compare their data and opinions with our own, and explore the gaps between the two perspectives. We should then reach out to the other side—that is, if we want to open the dialogue—and then set up the process of "synergy."

Many of us have ears to hear, but all too often, we don't really listen.

Step Three: Establish Impact

In Step Three, *we light the torch of enlightenment;* we "reframe" the topic and the needs. In short, we allow everyone to take one step back and to the side, so we can consider this topic from the other person's shoes. Within Step Three, we attempt to "unfreeze" perceptions, beliefs, and assumptions and to allow the data from Step Two to sink in and get our attention. This, in turn, allows us to form new impressions. This is the "ah-ha" step, as we need to look for something that will surprise or create "positive doubt" about current reality, practices, and perceptions. From our observations, most of us are good at "telling" the impact, but we need practice at facilitating so that people can internalize it.

Step Three is the "right brain" of the coaching process, in that we are attempting to creatively help others visualize and transcend time, position, and roles. Development occurs when introspection and curiosity are aroused.

Flexibility increases when people recognize and appreciate the impact of past choices and behaviors. Step Three is like stepping to the opening of a long, dark tunnel. You can see the world a lot better when you have a broad focus, rather than simply having deep "tunnel vision."

This is a step that cannot be forced.

With a broad perspective, you can decide whether change or status quo is the best approach. The constructive tension that is created when we take a broader view creates the internal motivation to 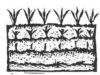 change. The true impact may soak in only after time has passed. You have to plant the seeds and let the new insights grow.

Constructive reflection enables the paradigm shift that is so critical to effective dialogue.

This step can create some discomfort as the "perception filters" come off and we begin to mentally get out of our comfort zone. This must take place before concrete actions, decisions, and resolutions can occur.

Step Three generates the deep inner power of coaching. **It doesn't involve doing things to people. It simply involves raising consciousness.**

As with all of the steps, Step Three has two edges. Both or all parties must cease to be locked into a partial picture of current reality. Our perceptual maps and beliefs of the situation are always a bit out of focus. With new insights, we can review our past assumptions and perceptions, then determine what we can do about them in light of what we want.

Step Four: Initiate a Plan

"Initiate" doesn't mean tell, sell, or dictate a plan.

In describing this vital step, we are not suggesting that the person who initiated the coaching necessarily be the one to actually produce the plan. From our perspective, we see co-producers. If you are really involved in a coaching dialogue, there is no way that you or the other party(s) can know the plan, decision, resolution or agreement until you have successfully traversed Steps Two and Three: DEFINING THE TOPICS AND NEEDS, and ESTABLISHING IMPACT.

The goal of this step is not only to seek immediate "technical" solutions to problems, but to seek out long-range opportunities that help develop skill and confidence among the participants, and enhance self-esteem. It is important that we don't manipulate or try to trick others into thinking that the suggested plan is theirs when it isn't. We should take enough time with this step to exercise the ideas, solutions, and options under consideration.

This step is the "brain" of the coaching model. Initiating a plan, involves throwing the critical questions out on the table for discussion. These include asking who will do what, where it will take place, and when. We should brainstorm on how to sort out the best decisions, options, and strategies. As a coach, there are times when you will pioneer or champion some starter ideas and become a catalyst.

The key here is boundary leadership: figuring out the legitimate constraints, resources, and objectives of your plan, and then setting out on the journey.

Step Five: Get a Commitment

In sequence, we could say that Step Three involves the decision to take a given journey. Step Four, the plan, becomes the road map for the journey, and Step Five is the heart, passion, or perseverance to get it started! Step Four looks at what is possible, Step Five looks at what is probable. People can do amazing things; the question we must ask is, "will they do the amazing?"

Whatever decisions, conclusions, plans, or agreements are arrived at, there needs to be *commitment.* Even if the coaching partners decide to give the situation more consideration, or to leave things as they are, some acknowledgment is needed. The key to this step is the process of building commitment, which depends largely on how well the other coaching steps have been followed.

> **If the plan, impact, topic, need, and support have been well established, then building commitment may be as simple as asking the question. If the prior steps have been a struggle, then building a commitment will be crucial and will take time, patience, and skill.**

Commitment is incremental.

Often, the commitment-building process is incremental, coming in stages until the other person becomes more comfortable with his or her involvement in the plan. The key is to offer several choices, draw out the commitment, and then hold this commitment up for scrutiny. This step is designed to bolster and "shore up" the integrity of the deal or plan that is decided upon. As a coach, you need to reveal your own commitment and enthusiasm.

We have observed that coaching survey scores are often noticeably lower on this step, when compared to Step Four. Your hard work on a plan should be matched in achieving a commitment. In other words, you need the "brain" (Step Four) and the "heart" (Step Five) in order to keep the coaching process going.

This step is not complicated or involved. The problem is that it is often ignored or forgotten.

The key to this step is to see if everyone is prepared and has the conviction to make something happen. This step begins with you—looking at your own passion for your part of the plan and what you can personally contribute. The commitment step is not designed to simply appease one party or another. As a coach, you should not be afraid of being a little redundant. Asking your partner to quantify the commitment level is very useful.

Step Six: Confront Excuses and Resistance

The tone of this step may sound a little harsh and insensitive. We likely named it as we did simply for effect, and to get attention. We know, from experience, that actions and agreements take a great deal of courage. Whenever we are dealing with important plans, topics, and agreements, there will always be hesitation and resistance to future and unknown courses of action. Excuses, resistance, and complaining could occur at the start, during, or even after the conversations.

Don't assume the placement of this step represents its likely occurrence.

At this point, the commitment process looks turbulent. As with the other steps, the commitment process requires patience from both parties. Too many excuses may be a signal that impact has not yet been achieved and that the plan and commitment may not be as solid as anticipated. Confronting the excuses and resistance starts the process of becoming free from the paralyzing grip.

Resistance is nature's way of telling us that we are on the right track, and that some turbulence is in the air.

Excuses are nothing more than limitations that both parties need to confront. You can free yourself from this drag by becoming more creative and courageous. Excuses simply mean that you need to redefine the plan, decision, or agreement.

Excuses and resistance force us to rethink the nature of the plan, and to create something that is workable for all parties involved. Excuses or resistance means a larger underlying issue needs to be addressed; for example, fear and anxiety of moving into new ground.

As coach, it is important to stay in touch with your own reservations and excuses, along with those of the other person—even though the other's resistance is easier to see than your own. As humans, we all have reservations, concerns, and fears that need to be taken into account. The way we manage these is to direct our resistance or excuse back to the plan, where we can generate preventions and contingencies that will help alleviate the resistance, fear, or conflict that has presented itself. We must also reassure each other with support and encouragement.

Step Seven: Clarify Consequences; Don't Punish

Information, not hardball conversation

With this step, we are not talking about promises; rather, we are talking about probabilities.

This step is the "what if" part of the coaching process. It focuses on the outcomes and what happens if the plan doesn't work. This is information, not discipline, hardball conversation, or threats. The words here are simple and logical, allowing for clarification without intimidation.

The key to successfully implementing this step is to look at the logical and natural outcomes first, before looking at position or political power, or even the ability of one person or another, to impose certain positive or negative consequences within his or her control. This step is important to unlocking motivational power. Whether we like it or not, most of us ask the question, *"What's in it for me?"* It is fair to answer this question, both for the other person as well as for yourself. If coaching solutions are to work, they must work for both parties.

A coach does not have to get into the "promise-making game." One simply has to look at the probabilities. This is how we offset the risks that either party may perceive in attempting to implement the coaching solution, plan, or agreement.

Step Eight: Don't Give Up

This final step is actually the "follow-through" step. It is the coach's "commitment." Designed to keep the process going, it demonstrates a tough inner core to the coaching process.

The message is simply this:
"How can the parties keep helping, teaching, and supporting each other in order to make the plan and the relationship work?"

At the tangible level, the parties need to review and rehearse the immediate next steps in the action plan. In a larger sense, this becomes the opportunity to "shore up" the relationship.

Celebration is the key to this step: the parties need to plan and anticipate the opportunity to recognize and celebrate the first steps toward progress. Some have shared with us that this step is the *beginning* of coaching and constructive dialogue, rather than the ending. The color of this step ties in with the heart of our model: SUPPORT. On a tangible level, the parties need to agree to the next time and place to meet and review the progress, changes, and improvements that are needed.

Coaching

What It Is

- A learnable skill
- Highly effective
- A process
- Requires patience
- Values driven
- Common sense
- Practical
- Useful for all team members
- A developmental process
- Builds on strengths
- Both "formal and ad hoc"
- A choice
- Proactive
- Dialogue, collaboration, and learning
- Useful in groups
- Verb: Dynamic/Action

What It Is Not

- A "genetic" gift
- Something that works every time
- An event
- A quick fix
- Techniques
- Common practice
- Just a "top-down" process
- Just "problem focused"
- A one-time, across-the-board "program"
- Automatic
- Reactive
- Control, order, and compliance
- Not just "one to one"
- Noun: Thing/Object

A simple dichotomy helps in trying to better understand coaching. Coaching is a learnable skill, not a genetic "gift" that people are born with. Coaching is a highly effective communication framework, although it is not something that works every time.

The coaching process must be examined as just that—a *process*—and not as a single event. It requires significant patience, and is not simply a "QUICK FIX." Coaching is built on a set of values, more than on a set of techniques, tricks, strokes, or manipulations to get people to do what is desired of them. In many ways, coaching is based upon common sense and is very practical in many of life's situations. Still, the problem is that IT IS NOT COMMON PRACTICE IN MOST GROUPS.

Coaching is not a "quick fix."

Coaching is useful for all members of an organization, regardless of their rank or office, and is not simply a management "thing" to be used in a "top-down" way! Coaching is used to build upon strengths that presently exist, while identifying and developing new ones. It is not simply a process to "fix" problems.

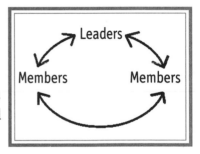

Coaching is both formal and informal, rather than a new *program*. Coaching is something the involved parties decide upon, and it cannot be simply forced into an organization. The major objectives of coaching are dialogue, collaboration, and learning, rather than trying to Control people, Order them, or Pressure them into compliance (C.O.P. Approach). It is very useful in group situations, as well as in one-on-one encounters. Coaching tries to achieve alignment, enhanced responsibility, and accountability. It is not a soft approach to relationships, where you allow people to do whatever they want—either to you, or to the organization as a whole.

Coaching works best when people use it as a pro-active method, rather than in reaction to situations that are becoming difficult.

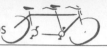

Finally, as you think about the coaching model, try to think of coaching situations like a combination lock. Each step represents a number in the combination. Each situation may require just a little different code or combination, depending on the people involved. You have to figure out the precise pattern to unlock a step and achieve a win-win solution. The combination is always changing. Listen to the signals, get to know your partner, learn how to dial up the code, relax, and don't force it.

When you learn the coaching combination you are able to prepare for the future, learn from the past, and truly live in the present.

Chapter 6
The Miner's Quarter:

**A Real-Life Story of Synergistic Coaching
in Action**

Chapter 6
The Miner's Quarter:
A Real-Life Story of Synergistic Coaching in Action

Along the western slope of the Rocky Mountains in Colorado, the face of the rugged landscape is pocked by the mark of the prospector. Derelict mines dot the land. Dark, open wounds in the sides of the mountains gape silently, withholding their secrets about who disappeared into them or whether their treasure had ever been yielded up.

As sudden as snake holes, as curious as bullet holes, each mine harbors a mystery. Some stare from rock so sheer as to defy entrance, while others yawn at the end of a switch-back trail on gentler slopes. Mines, wherever you come upon them, conjure images of hearty and adventurous men with picks, shovels, and guns—the tools that conquered the old west.

To the clinking music of the pick-axe, thousands staked their claims, assayed, chipped, and dug. Some won, some lost. Mines swallowed lives whole. Few enjoyed a longer, more productive history than the "Lady Luck" mine, which is still in operation not far from Durango. So many mines were shut down by competition that came with new technology and modern management skills. For the "Lady," as the miners call her, luck has been both good and bad. But she has survived.

When I took over as supervisor at the "Lady Luck," I already knew she had a history of trouble. An adversarial relationship had existed between managers and workers for a long time. They lived in two separate worlds—one, above ground in well-lighted, air-conditioned offices; the other, hundreds of feet down, entombed in darkness, two worlds divided by more than mere physical distance. Though it had been a while since the miners had chosen to strike and morale was on the upswing, the miners themselves were neither highly productive nor very safety conscious.

Located high in a box canyon, the "Lady Luck" was a large mine with plenty of gold left in her. More than a century of digging and hauling had sent her shafts deep into a rugged peak called Iron Mountain, which was rich in ore of several kinds. Miners have a kind of love-hate relationship with "The Lady," because of the hard work she demands. They enter her dark shafts early in the morning, before sunup, and don't come out until evening, usually after the sun has set. The work is long and arduous—muscles strain and tools break against the hard rock, lungs ache in the stale air, and stress can build like atmospheric pressure when you're a mile deep in the earth. As rough as it is, though, when a miner sees a gleaming bar of pure gold bullion, he feels the satisfying pleasure of teamwork, and feels he's making a contribution not only with his own paycheck but to society as a whole. The miners are proud to produce gold, the mineral that says wealth and prosperity in any language.

Conditions had improved considerably at the mine when I began supervising, but even though we've become both safer and more productive, we still have a ways to go. There are still old habits to break, old ways to change. And I can think of no better example of the need for change at the mine than Fred. A tough and well-seasoned old-timer, Fred has survived the risky life of a miner for twenty-six years and takes everything as it comes.

Every miner is a gambler at heart. Like so many whose jobs are dangerous, Fred has come to terms with the fact that no matter how careful you are, there are times when disaster is beyond your control. In Fred's terms, "When you're number's up, it's up. That's all." And because of this somewhat callused view, Fred has become casual about certain safety procedures and general housekeeping.

Like any skilled worker, Fred knows the short-cuts that save time in his work, making him more productive. Paid for what he produces, in addition to his hourly wage, a miner can make a lot more by working fast. Unfortunately, some of the corners Fred chose to cut reduced security, and exposed others to accidents—like not using enough of the six-foot bolts to stabilize new cuts in the stope, the work area. His disregard for some procedures had been reported to me, and though it seems justifiable to him, the problem is that Fred is a crew leader. His crew follows the standard he sets, so the potential for accidents gets multiplied.

One day, in an attempt to work with Fred a bit on his laxness, I went down to his area, deep in the mine. He works almost a mile underground, on what we call the 5250 level. Fred and his crew work in an isolated area, and it didn't surprise me when I walked into it and found tools strewn about in rubble that hadn't been cleared away. I also noticed several frayed electrical wires, and the biggest concern of all in a mine shaft, missing bolts. These long metal rods were driven into the stope in a four-foot square pattern, with a bolt in each corner and one in the center, to stabilize the newly cut areas. Rock is full of faults and fissures, and is only as secure as its weakest vein, so the bolts become vital to security.

Through a connecting tunnel, I found Fred and called, "Hey, Fred, got a minute?"

"Sure, Chuck. You're the boss," came his response with a condescending edge.

I smiled and joked with him, adding "But do you think that really makes any difference?"

He smiled back, but didn't want to give too much. Then he asked with a hint of a patronizing tone, "So, Chuck, what can we do for you today?"

"Oh, not much," I responded. "Just wanted to ask you a couple quick things." I paused, looked around us. Noticing that only four bolts were used in what should have been a five-bolt pattern right next to us, I continued, "Fred, if a three-foot by three-foot rock popped out 'o this wall where that bolt is missing, what do you think it would do to you if it got you?"

Fred looked at me with a steely, steady gaze. It was a look that said that he had thought about it and dismissed it already, "I'd be smashed like an ant."

I thought to myself, Perfect! Exactly! I've got him where I want him. But I didn't want to agree too enthusiastically for fear of offending him. I tried another question, "Fred, how *would* you react if something like that really happened to you?"

He looked hard at me and slipped his large, rough hands into the pockets of his soiled, gray coveralls.

I feared I had come on too strong, making him feel guilty or bad. But to my surprise he pulled a quarter out of his pocket and rolled it around in his hand. Then with the end of his thumb, he flipped the quarter in the air toward me. My reflexes snatched it in mid-air. Giving him a puzzled look, I asked, "What's this for, Fred?"

In his cool, matter-of-fact tone, he said, "Chuck, why don't you call somebody who gives a... somebody who cares?" With hands on his hips and a stern expression on his dirt-stained face, Fred stared me down, the light on his helmet bright in my face.

Nothing else was said, and I left, astonished. Speechless, I rode the elevator to the surface and a moment later walked from the mine into the light of day still stunned, wondering at what had just happened. How could Fred not be concerned about his own safety? Then, all at once it hit me. Fred's a miner. Been here a long time. Has the old view, the outmoded paradigm. And I just got the brush off. He really *doesn't* care what happens to him. How do you get to somebody like that? How could I get through?

My first thought was, *Why should I even keep him around? I ought to can him right now!*

The more I thought about it, the more I realized something that *did* matter to Fred. More than the mine, more than anything, Fred loves the little farm where he works on weekends and holidays. I recalled him telling me that he was saving up to buy a new tractor. Could it be that Fred's drive for higher production was to earn money for that tractor, and that he was seeing himself get closer to earning the money for it every time he rushed through procedures? Could that be a reason for his apparent disregard for safety? It really does take a little more time and effort to comply, maybe that was it. I resolved to talk to him again.

Early the next morning, I headed down to 5250 again. Instinctively, the conversation that ran through my mind on the elevator was a shouting match between Fred and me, but I really wanted to have a good talk with him. Maybe even get him to think of the possibilities. As I entered his work area, the scene was familiar—hard work in progress but little concern for safety and order. At that level, the heat of the earth increases, but I wasn't sure that my own temperature wasn't rising too. As a perfectionist, I had to summon my patience. So I spent a minute chatting with a few crew members about how the equipment was running. They always like to talk about the task they're on. Even when they're complaining you can tell they love what they're talking about—getting the job done, staying on task, keeping the production going. Soon they stopped work for a smoke break.

I strolled over to Fred, who sat alone. He looked up at me and asked with a sweaty grin, his teeth white beneath the smudge he wore like a permanent tattoo, "Did ya call anybody interested?"

"No," I chuckled back, "but I did buy a cup of coffee with your quarter, thanks."

"I'm glad you did something constructive with it," he returned. Then he added "You management types need the money."

I stayed calm and said, "Fred, let me ask you a little bit of a different question if I can. If we had a federal mine inspector walk in here right now and do a review on our operation, what kind of recommendations do you think we would get?"

He looked up and said through a thoughtful smile, "You know, Chuck, you got a good point. I think if I was an MSHA inspector and walked in here right now, I'd slap a big red shut-down tag on us."

"Really?" I said. "Why do you think we should be shut down?"

"Well, Chuck, it's like you said yesterday, we got a few bolts missing here and there . . . but basically things are staying together. A technicality from my point of view, but still, I think the mine inspector should shut us down. We got a little housekeeping we need to do. We have a couple of wires that need to be spliced and repaired but I think if he's doing his job, he ought to shut us down."

Again, I thought, *Perfect! Exactly! Even stronger than what I would have said.* I thought we might get a citation, but Fred is saying they would shut us down. So, I ventured my next question: "Fred, what's that going to do to your paycheck? And what would that do to our mine's profitability? What about our ability to compete and be the low-cost producer in the state?"

Fred thought a moment. He seemed to be considering what I was asking. It seemed he might be adjusting his opinion until his hands went for his pockets. Another quarter. His thumb flicked it in a high arch toward me and again I caught it in mid-air.

This time I tried to get a jump on Fred and asked, "Who do you want me to call this time, Fred?"

He droned, and stared into his coffee cup, "Anybody you want."

It seemed strange. Here I was trying, with all my might to connect with Fred, trying to support him, controlling myself so I wouldn't yell, and it wasn't working. He seems capable of only seeing issues one way—the way he's seen them for the last twenty-six years. How could I expect Fred to ever reason with me? Isn't there a way to get Fred out of the box that limits his perceptions to recognize the risks to his own productivity, his own paycheck?

I found myself considering Fred from another perspective. I had been wrong about what motivated him. It hadn't been his eagerness for earning a new tractor that pushed him to ignore safety procedures, and it wasn't within his range of concerns to worry deeply about the mine's competitive position. My approaches had missed the mark with this man. He was a survivor. He doesn't need this mine to meet his income needs every month. His wife and kids all work part-time, and if there was a shutdown that put workers out for any period of time, Fred would go work the farm. He might even prefer that. As a union member and an activist on the side that opposed business and management, Fred likely would see a shutdown as good. Besides getting a lot done on the farm, he could even get some unemployment benefits. He probably feels that the company is making too much profit as it is.

Thinking about Fred in this way aroused all my old authoritarian tendencies and control methods. I had to fight the urge to punish him by just handing him a pink slip right then and there. Maybe it would be better for both him and us if he did leave the mine for something he loved more, and he could just farm full time. Should I give him a couple of days off to think about it?

Suddenly, it occurred to me what I was doing. If I wanted Fred to abandon an attitude that was destructive or unproductive, I must recognize my own behaviors and attitudes that needed changing. I started seeing my own desires to control Fred as destructive and began coaching myself toward more of a win-win perspective. I asked myself why he was working here, what he's committed to, who he's loyal to, what interests him, and in fact, what made him get up in the morning.

What my "coaching" questions revealed was the other side of Fred, a side I had been ignoring. He likes people and issues. He has service on some union committees, and he has always been willing to take new employees under his wing while they learned the ropes. Fred sees himself as a mentor, willing to train, teach, and help. I know he's a good father and that his children love and respect him. He is a role model here at the mine, even though some of his behaviors are a bit risky.

With this new understanding of Fred moving around in my head, I also realized that Fred was not willingly committed to safety, and despite any efforts I might employ to force good safety practices, I could never successfully control his conduct. It's impossible for me to be everywhere—to watch, to check, to legislate positive attitudes and actions that comply with rules and policies. But at the same time, there was no question that Fred was a productive miner, a tough case, but good for the job.

That week, as I checked with others who had worked with him, I was able to confirm that he enjoys a role in the development of workers. Underneath the rhetoric and his hard shell, Fred was not as tough as he wanted to portray. I realized I had to help him relax and not feel defensive or threatened by my interest in him. I wanted to convey to him that we were on the same side.

As I walked up to him the next time I saw him, I could tell he knew what was on my mind. His subtle humor led him to put his hands in his pockets and rattle his change. I tried a whole new direction, no controls. "Fred, could I get you a cup of coffee?" I asked as I pulled out my quarters.

"Sure, no problem," he answered. "What can I do for you, Chuck?"

"Not much. I'm wondering if you have an opinion about how the new miners are doing. Do you think we're hiring the right type of guy?"

Fred had already been thinking. "Well, at first I had my doubts. They're a little slow and I wasn't sure they are tough enough. You know how kids are these days."

"I sure do," I said, "good help is hard to find."

"Yeah, but they're coming along. Give me a little more time with them, and I'll make miners out of 'em yet," he added.

I could feel my approach was right, this time. I went on: "Tell me a little bit about Pat. How long has he worked with you?"

"Pat's only been here about nine months. You can't expect too much out of him yet. It took a while just to build up Pat's endurance, but he's come a long way. I think if you stay off our case, we'll make Pat a miner yet."

I looked at Fred through new eyes that day and liked what I saw. "Sounds good. Fred, I have a lot of confidence in your ability to teach him the cuttling and mucking end of the business. How well do you think Pat understands our back-up procedures? Does he know our safe areas and rescue procedures if we have some kind of accident down here?"

"Well, to be honest with you, Chuck, I think he's a little weak in that area. Like I said earlier, he has only been here nine months. It's taken me twenty-six years to get to know this mine and I know it like the back of my hand. It'll take Pat a bit of time, but I could teach him our rescue procedures in a week and give him that routine."

"Tell me if I have this right," I said. "In the worst-case scenario, if a cave-in occurred today, you wouldn't have any trouble getting out of here, would you?"

"No, not really, I've been here a while."

"You know, Fred, if I were a betting person, I would bet a huge sum of money that any time we have an accident, you would figure out a way to beat the odds. You're tough, smart, and determined to survive." I paused.

Fred responded sarcastically, "Aw, Chuck, that's the sweetest thing you ever said about me. Thank you."

Then I moved in a bit. "What about Pat? Do you think that if a big one hit today…well, what kind of odds would you put on his getting out of here alive?"

Silence.

"Suppose a missing bolt… uh, if a big cave-in breaks loose and these missing bolts cause this section to fail, Pat would be crushed. Fred, you and I would have to visit his home. We'd need to visit the home of anyone who didn't survive."

"What do you mean, Chuck?" he asked with concern.

"Well, as a lead miner and as mine superintendent, I think we would have an obligation to go see Pat's family."

"You mean, at their house?" He was genuinely surprised.

"That's the usual procedure—at least two people from the company need to visit the homes, explain what happened… Fred, I was wondering if you could help me a bit. Let's just suppose for a minute that we're standing on Pat's front porch. Let's figure out how we're going to handle this. We knock, someone from Pat's family, say, maybe one of his kids or his wife, maybe his brother or sister, comes to the door. They don't look surprised. In fact, they look pretty calm. What do we say?"

There was a long silence as Fred contemplated all this. Finally, he couldn't contain it, "What do you mean, what will we say?"

"What I mean is how do we start this, how do we explain this loss to the family?" I added. Silence. "Fred, what reason or what excuse can we give the family members to help them feel better?" Longer silence. In my training I had discovered the powerful gauge that silence is. I let it work, tempted to comment and grind my point in. But I gave Fred the space he needed.

Finally, I added, "Fred, listen. Give it some thought. I've never had to do it either. I just know that in the miner's code of our company policy, we are specified as the ones to deliver the news to the family. I'll be honest, I don't know how to do it and I never want to learn how. That's why I follow all the safety steps. Let's talk in a couple of days, shall we?" I left quickly before Fred could argue.

Knowing I was bucking decades of experience, I didn't expect much very fast. I didn't expect any of what happened the next time I saw Fred. When I walked into his area a week later, I was not prepared for what I saw. I surveyed the scene. The housekeeping had been done, the drills, the bits, and other tools were all properly stored. Electrical cords that had been frayed were now spliced, taped, and mended—hanging in loops on the wall rack. All five bolts appeared in each of the support patterns along the walls. Rubble had been cleared, and the place was transformed.

"Hey, Fred," I called, trying to remain calm, "how's it going?" It was hard to hold back my pride and a grin.

With a new tone in his voice, Fred said, "You tell me."

After genuinely commending him and his crew, we discussed the effort. As we started to part, Fred added, "But you can't have every-thing."

I asked, "What does that mean?"

"Well, we lost a couple tons of production in the catching up we had to do here."

This was an important moment to share with Fred what really mattered in this whole exchange. "Fred, I want to be real clear about this," I began. "I think it is important but I don't want to have to make people do it. What do you and the rest of the team members think? Is this important?"

Fred's response was honest. "Chuck, we're not absolutely convinced and I would be lying if I said we were. But hey, listen. We may not be setting production records every week. If you can live with that, we can live with spending a little bit more time on safety."

"Listen, Fred, that sounds good to me. I just think we have two jobs to do out here—two missions in life. One is to mine this ore productively, and the other is to stay in business without chopping off legs and hurting people," I explained.

"That is sort of the conclusion I came to, too. But don't spread it around that I'm getting soft. I've built my reputation being a hard-nosed miner and want to keep it that way," Fred said with a small laugh.

"Fred, I don't think you are ever going to hear me say you are a soft miner, but just don't think that being a safe miner means that you are soft. I think this is the environment that I would like to see our new employees trained in. People need to learn what it means to work hard and work safe. I just talked to the personnel department, and they've got a couple of new trainees that need to be broken in. Would you be willing to take them on?"

Fred rubbed his strong, square jaw, then ran his fingers through his wiry hair. Finally he declared, "Well, Chuck, I'm willing to at least talk to them. Like I have always said, they've got to have the right stuff. If they don't have the right stuff, I don't want them in my area."

"That sounds fair enough to me," I returned. "Why don't you stop by the conference room at the end of the shift and talk to them for a few minutes, then tell us what you think. And by the way, Fred, here are a couple quarters. Get your guys a cup of coffee on break."

Tilting his head playfully, Fred added, "You know, Chuck, I was wondering when you were ever going to loosen up and do something for us. I guess you're not half bad, after all."

Just hearing these words made the effort worth it. I said, "See you in a week... keep up the good work!"

Chapter 7
Step One:
Be Supportive

Simply put, supportiveness *is not* an option when it comes to coaching. The success of a coaching discussion...is determined by the level of support.

The Coach

Chapter 7
Step One: Be Supportive

Now we would like to explore each of these steps in greater depth. This section reaches into the far recesses of the model and provides a more substantial well-spring of understanding of these crucial ingredients of synergistic partnerships.

As you read the pages that follow, we recommend that you read one or two chapters at a sitting. Take time to digest and ponder the various facets of the model. By reading in this manner, you will find yourself both *enjoying* and *metabolizing* the points of the coaching mosaic.

Whenever a "feeling" or "sensitive dimension" of communications is mentioned, some people become "queasy" or uncomfortable. It doesn't have to be that way. Support doesn't have to be a "touchy-feely" thing that makes more "task-oriented" people uneasy.

At the very deepest level, support is all about helping others get what they want and need.

Acceptance and understanding are the foundation of synergistic relationships. Support is not saying clever or charming things at a superficial level and then turning into a "piranha" when the pressure, emotions, and fear build up. Simply put, if you demonstrate a commitment to help people get what they need, you are being supportive. And if what they need is at all in common with the needs of the team or yourself, then being supportive takes on a "win-win" significance. Support becomes a strategic part of the task when you facilitate the way to more success and learning.

We never outgrow our need to receive and to give support.

We may, however, outgrow patience; and we may become forgetful and even move into a denial mode with regard to support. One tough client put it this way: "Listen, I want you to understand a couple of things. First of all, I don't need support because I get loved at home. If you feel you need a friend, I suggest that you buy a dog, because in my opinion, the only place you will find compassion around here is in a dictionary."

Support—A Universal Need

Whether this individual cares to admit it or not, we all need support. We may each prefer different kinds and different times frames, but we all need it at one time or another. As with all of coaching, try to look at giving support as your own personal choice. You can't wait until it is politically correct. Even in a culture where support may not be in vogue. If you do, you are giving up all of the advantages that come from your support being genuine and spontaneous. Your companions and partners in life can recognize the difference. They will appreciate you, and they will respond to your caring intentions.

Relationships and interaction, like life, are fragile and temporary. The people we live and work with simply won't be around forever! Therefore, we must be careful that we value and appreciate individuals for who they are, as well as for what they contribute.

It seems that every day we see and experience the harsh realities of life; and we deal with people who are truly not very supportive of us. We may also encounter individuals who do not need a lot of support from us, whether it is the taxi driver or the server at our favorite fast food restaurant. These

So, in our own way—and depending on the other person—we must find a way to be supportive.

relationships are quick and instrumental. It is essential that we don't create "fast food" relationships with people who can play a role in our life.

Still, the relationships we truly care so much about—at home, at work, in the classroom, or in the organization—are deserving of support.

The key is to simply give that support, either in a reserved and "responsible" manner, or in an open and unrestrained way. The key is to do whatever works for you and the personality style of your partner. Ask those around you whether they feel supported. If you take a quiet moment with them, and if you are patient, they will tell you. Be open to the need for some adjustment in the way you support others. Sometimes, when we get into the coaching dialogue, we discover that we are doing exactly what we had decided <u>not</u> to do. Don't be too hard on yourself; listen to feedback from others and adjust your behavior to support their needs.

The need for support can be bottomless, and rarely can one individual give another all of the support that is needed in life. If people become dependent on only one or two persons for their primary source of support, the support giver becomes worn out. One of the most helpful ways to assist and enrich the experiences of your partners is to coach them into developing multiple relationships and multiple sources of support.

The key to good partnerships and good interaction is balance. Support can be balanced with the expectation of more accountability and responsibility. An imbalance in favor of support is indulgent and may even be counterproductive. Likewise, in the absence of support, accountability, and responsibility become harsh and even intimidating. As a result, fear and defensiveness begin to emerge, and constructive openness begins to close.

If they feel accepted and understood, they will trust your intentions to help and be more trusting in return. The key is to be open and honest about your support. If a situation develops that gives you mixed feelings, simply say, "This part makes me feel "X" (excited, pleased, comfortable) and this part of the situation leaves me feeling "Y" (confused, frustrated, worried). They will open their minds and work with you to create cooperation and synergy.

If the people you are with don't feel attacked or "pinned down," they can relax and open up.

Support Defined

Sometimes we are asked if Step One, *Support*, is really a step that requires a specific act, or if it is simply the climate or the character of the relationship. The answer is simple: Support is all of these! It requires specific, interactive behaviors, as well as consistent, positive, and ongoing behavior.

Support skills can be developed much like the other skills in the coaching process. In India, the cow is regarded as sacred, and in the coaching model, Step One holds a very special place! It is respectfully placed in the middle of the coaching model because of the key role it plays setting up and triggering recurring positive moments between coaching partners. It must be consistent and genuine.

Support is both an attitude and a set of behaviors that demonstrate the desire to create collaborative partnerships with others.

We sometimes are asked whether Step One is more important than the other steps. To us, it is like asking whether eyes are more important than ears, or whether the heart is more important than the brain. The elements of the coaching model have a symbiotic relationship with each other. If the coaching relationship is to grow and flourish, it has to have fertile soil and lots of sunshine and water.

Clearly, without support, a relationship won't grow and our interactions are one-way and mechanical.

From a base of support, you can spring into other steps, and from other steps, you can return to "support" in order to help keep the interaction in perspective.

Successful coaching relationships take a very large amount of support. Supportive, nurturing, and caring behaviors are central to a synergistic partnership. We call support "Step One"—not because this is where you must start (although it is a good place to begin), but the other elements of the coaching model will be effective to the degree that "support" is firmly rooted.

It sounds easy, but thousands of observations in our coaching seminars have led us to believe that expressing a supportive, or "feeling" statement, or behaving supportively can be difficult. Support may mean more to some of our coaching partners than to others. The upside gain that can come from support far outweighs the risk of causing harm from too much support! For every complaint we hear of someone being too supportive, we hear 99 complaints of people who are insensitive and negative.

Be willing to "toe the mark."

Support as a Core Value

Non-supportive personality types argue that compassion and support get in the way of good judgment. They may have a point—if they are doing the judging. However, if you are attempting to enroll, collaborate with, and develop others, support becomes a necessary ingredient of the coaching process.

At its deepest core, support is a personal value and characteristic.

For some individuals, support is a natural step: it is almost as if it is in their genes. For others, support is a conscious choice.

It doesn't matter whether support comes easy or hard. Ultimately, it has to come from the heart. You must be sincere. You can't pretend to be supportive for long and get away with it. The people you work with will eventually see through pretense. Support cannot be a predictable set of behaviors, or customs, that you merely follow by rote. Cosmetic hugs and kisses, in anticipation of a return for your charming ways, will label you as a manipulator. Webster uses the word *obsequious* to describe this behavior. Someone who is obsequious is "falsely polite; a person with a velvet tongue."

> Support must be a lot more than just saying nice things.

People around you constantly form impressions about the nature and extent of your support. These impressions will influence their efforts and the extent of their openness to you. All of this makes support a slippery concept. If you achieve only a shallow level of "popular" support, you will lose the potential benefits available to you. If your support is genuine and deep, you can accomplish long term openness, dialogue, and understanding. There are times when giving support means telling the truth, even though it may initially hurt.

If you falsely tell people what they want to hear, or make up stories and compromise the truth, you set yourself up for a breach of trust.

Honesty, with the intention of helping, is the highest form of support, even though it doesn't always produce "thank you's" and immediate affection.

Eventually, however, it will lead to the respect and dignity the relationship deserves. If people believe that you are interested in and supportive of them for what they do, as well as for who they are—for their inner strengths, such as their loyalty, beliefs, and intentions—you will begin to fill a support "reservoir" with your associates and partners.

If you are to be genuine with support, you must be a good observer and have a basic understanding of human behavior. You can build an effective pillar of support if you can understand what others want and need: for example, their financial and career needs, as well as their emotional needs to belong, to be heard, to be respected, and to be involved. People appreciate you more if you support their need for reassurance, for approval, and to not feel totally alone on a topic.

Effective support can be achieved through the recognition and affirmation of an individual. However, you must also remember and respect each person's individual differences. For example, some people are embarrassed by recognition or by receiving public credit.

You can create a strong foundation for your relationships if others can see your actions and feel your spirit through non-verbal communications. Support does not necessarily mean agreement or approval of another person's choices or actions. You can empathize and understand or support people without being their best friend or by agreeing with them on every point. Support goes way beyond a specific issue, position, or individual belief.

To illustrate this, we have a trusted colleague and trusted coach who is in a marriage, as well as a business relationship, in which he and his wife and his best friend and partner often arrive at an impasse in their decision-making. When this occurs, they have adopted the notion that "It is okay to agree to disagree" without becoming a disagreeable personality. Respect for the other person's position is always possible: agreement is not. They have given each other permission to feel "safe and unthreatened" in their respective relationships, while maintaining their own beliefs on a given issue. In this man's marriage, he refers to this moment as "holy deadlock!" Because both he and his partner are football fanatics, they refer to it as "holy gridlock!" It works for them, as they have given their differences a humorous "handle," and it may work effectively for you.

It is okay to agree to disagree.

The aim of this step in the coaching process is to create a greater level of respect and trust between the players in the partnership.

Support is designed to tranquilize defensiveness, fear, and resentment and to communicate confidence, to validate and maintain self-esteem, even in the midst of adversity.

Support can help when the parties are being stretched out of their comfort zones by new or exciting challenges.

When people are in one-on-one situations, they often report a mutually uncomfortable feeling: nervousness and an increase in anxiety. This can often lead to situations where individuals become resistant, defensive, and even cantankerous. If there is fear in the relationship, they will tend to run away and hide from growth opportunities, mistakes, and learning oppor-

Support is like a "safety net" for the unknown.

tunities. Support allows members of the organization to take reasonable risks.

Support is different from being "nice." Nice can be interpreted as superficial, while support is an enabler, leading to clarity, action, responsibility, and accountability.

Support as a Long-Term Investment

Think of support as an investment in the long-term relationship-building process, similar to investing in an oil change for your prized automobile. You really

can't see an immediate change in efficiency or fuel economy after the oil change, and going through the procedure of changing the oil costs money and time. Still, beneath the hood of your car, the pistons and valves are rejoicing! They appreciate the fact that they can continue working for thousands of miles. Support, then, is like fresh oil that is fed into the engines, eliminating the friction in your relationships. Its value is subtle and almost incalculable!

We have many friends who drive their "black and gummy oil" engines until their car almost throws a rod or grinds to an eventual stop. They give up on the maintenance because an immediate or dramatic return isn't visible and immediate. We need to trust the experts and researchers on automotive performance when they tell us that this procedure will significantly prolong the life of the vehicle and will keep it running efficiently.

Strong, ongoing support gives you the leeway to maintain cooperation when there isn't time to "change the oil" and you have to be direct and assertive. If the fresh "support oil" has been applied, people will not interpret your directness as hostile, aggressive, or demeaning, or as insensitivity, punishment, or rejection.

Support, by itself, may not buy you or your partners anything productive in the short run. Short-term thinkers may find this step frustrating. However, if you are in relationships and teamwork for the long run, you will see tremendous results as you work to create a culture of quality and empowerment. The ultimate outcome will be the creation of a team that cares about success and that enjoys the benefits of a productive team atmosphere.

Another goal of the support step is to help the other person relax and to reduce some of the anxiety when talking one-on-one.

With a safe and non-threatening environment, the other steps can be followed more easily and the dialogue can be allowed to unfold naturally. Nevertheless, support, respect, courtesy, and human sensitivity should not be confused with weakness, indecisiveness, poor judgment, or lack of firmness.

In a coaching dialogue, people must know when to provide more support and when the situation requires a firm and direct focus on another step. Being clear and direct, as well as supportive and caring, are simply two different things; they are not opposites or mutually exclusive. You can be both direct and supportive; your intentions and how the directness is communicated determine the meaning. Are your intentions to help or hurt, to explore or belittle, to learn or place blame? By being direct, you are implicitly saying, "This is the best way to make our conversation productive." If this is your intention, let the other person know it; the natural reaction is to impute negative intentions to directness. Do you

Be cautious; check perceptions.

Some misuse the **warrant** of openness and directness as a way to punish or pay back others for some unresolved issue or offense.

communicate your directness in a way that maintains the other person's dignity and worth? If not, your directness will rightfully be perceived as non-supportive. Being both direct and supportive is not a widely practiced skill.

If the idea of support appeals to you, think about how you can improve and polish your abilities and skills to line up with your supportive values and beliefs.

Don't assume just because the concept of support seems right to you that you are good at it.

When it comes to effective dialogue with others, people are willing to commit that extra discretionary performance only to the extent that they have trust and confidence in the relationship.

People simply do not respond in a genuine, good-faith, and sincere way to coaches whom they don't trust or whom they see as adversaries.

From time to time, you may need to ask yourself the question, "What have I really and honestly done with the relationship to create the bonds and develop some affinity between myself and the other person?" It takes more than routine or mundane support.

Try to be creative in the types and delivery of support.

Success with this concept will lower defensiveness, facilitate collaboration, and create a safe environment so that the truth can be explored and so new challenges and risks can be pursued to help empower our partners. Ignoring support, or being downright non-supportive, will lower the self-worth of the other person, creating doubt and a feeling of victimization. It may even kindle the desire to retaliate and lead to fear, withdrawal, and anger in both parties.

The How-To's of Support

The goal of support is simple: to establish some positive contact. Positive contact and positive experiences will lead to respect and honesty—a key operating fuel for relationships in any kind of organization. Support will not grow by sitting around and talking about it; we must actually "walk our talk." Support involves a whole range of behaviors, skills, and values.

Actions speak louder than words

There are many practical ways that you can go about creating more support with others. First of all, when you are around the people you care about, try to acknowledge their positive intentions. Your companions are with you because they want to be, and they are trying to do the right thing. View them as your allies. Sit down and talk to people. They will share with you the things they are doing to support the team. Build this alliance. They will also explain the obstacles, excuses, and problems hampering their efforts. Ninety-nine percent of the time, you can find something positive to build on in what they tell you and you will discover the silver lining of their intentions. Believe in their fundamental value and contributions.

Regardless of the level of result or accomplishment, make sure that you state your awareness of their positive intentions.

This can be a challenge when you are in the middle of a crisis, if you have a short emotional fuse, or if your problems have been left unattended over a period of time.

So think through support before you seek out the other person, and allow a little time to get a full perspective of the situation.

Part of what you may want to discuss may simply be that the other person has only a partial view of what needs to be achieved. Additionally, that person's actions may not be aligned with the intentions of the team, as a result of only seeing part of the whole picture. Herein lies your coaching opportunity to draw back the blinders supportively. Gently help the other person to see, and then invite them to join in with you in creating new expectations and intentions. Be willing to use the coaching process to fully discuss emerging needs and opportunities. Look at these as positive change opportunities.

Unfortunately, some writers are suggesting that good partners won't try to "change" you. We see it a little differently. Ignoring growth opportunities, positive changes, and problems leads to neglect and acceptance of mediocrity for both partners. This is quitting or giving up, which is the opposite of the last step in the coaching model. We believe the coaching process is a matter of timing, skill, and sincerity. In short, having high expectations is very supportive; just avoid impossible ones. Avoid expressing opportunities, expectations, or opportunities in a negative, put down fashion. Allow your partner to have and express expectations of you.

Be patient, and take your time.

If you focus too hard or too soon on the task, or on the harsh realities of the situation, you can easily put the other person on the defensive without really intending to. We are not suggesting that you have to drag your feet and look as if you are trying to avoid the issue. Be neither pusillanimous nor wishy-washy. Be honest and assertive when the time is right.

An essential key is to be prepared to be vulnerable yourself, to disclose what you struggle with in conjunction with the subject that you are discussing.

You may want to try a "coaching contract." Say to the person with whom you are coaching: "I am willing to work really hard to be open and listen. What do you think? Would this be good for both of us?"

"Own up" if you are pressed, challenged, puzzled, confused, frustrated, or in the dark as to essential information. The greatest fault of all is to be conscious of none. Owning up helps foster a safe environment for synergy and collaboration. Use non-threatening questions; then listen and express clear and non-punishing statements and opinions. You can gently focus and converge to the heart of the topic and the key underlying issues.

You can help maintain support if you can get your partner talking.

If the topic is creating defensiveness early on, then inject more support into the discussion. Begin with support and exercise patience and good coaching style to help develop, motivate, or inspire the other person to collaborate with you.

If you want to be aggressive, then be aggressive with support. Make sure you can hear it, put it into words, and follow-up with action. Don't make support an incidental or glancing blow, but score direct "hits," and let the other party know what you appreciate in him or her, and what works well for you. From this supportive foundation, the discussion of core issues or sensitive issues will be more productive. In fact, after your partner knows that you mean them no harm, and that you are in fact in favor of working through the situation together, he or she will respond in kind. If you can encourage your partner to talk, do so, and watch him or her open up and drive out the fear that may have been harbored. You will probably find that this approach brings immediate as well as long-term payoffs.

Go into the "support offensive" mode.

Lead-Off Questions

The following start-up questions work well, as you get a dialogue going in a supportive fashion:

- *What are your hopes and dreams for. . . ?*
- *What do you want from. . . ?*
- *How are your assignments and responsibilities going for you?*
- *What is working well, and what isn't working so well?*
- *What has been your experience with. . . ?*
- *What do you feel that you are good at?*
- *Do you trust me to help you with. . . ?*
- *Can I coach/support/mentor/guide you?*
- *Do you want to go to the next level of development?*
- *If you were to select something to work on, to improve, or to develop, what would that be?*

> If you have a problem to solve, you can't look too far into the past without sounding punitive; but with support, all the past successes will carry weight.

Once one or more of these questions are asked, it will be useful to look at the "big picture" and even to look into the past to find things to support. When you begin coaching, start with what is happening now that people have some control over. Most problems are created because the "system"—you and your partner all have a joint role in creating it. Don't overload your partner with all of the responsibility. We have a coaching colleague who states it this way: "Place blame on the situation, rather than on the person. This approach leaves the person's self-esteem intact." Look first at the process and procedures and then look at personal responsibility.

It is likewise helpful to learn to compartmentalize, to search for fair shares of the responsibility for a problem. Also, look for at least one thing—even a very small thing—that you can do to help them as you work through the plan of action. This helps to almost institutionalize the support. Keep responsibilities balanced. We are not suggesting that you put the action "monkey" entirely on the back of either person.

One important form of support is the values you display while talking with another person about any subject. An example might be the way you respect or disrespect others who are not in on the conversation. A second is the behavior that you engage in on a daily basis. These are sometimes the virtually invisible types of support that you communicate after you have made the decision to incorporate support as a part of your "style."

Remember that one of the highest forms of support (when coaching others) is to incorporate their views, their ideas, and then enroll them in providing a solution.

If support is a fundamental part of your daily routine and ongoing mode of operation, or part of your organization's culture, then it will <u>not</u> be perceived as merely cosmetic, manipulative, or phony.

Some suggestions to help you "walk your talk" and carry it over to your routine are as follows: Encourage an "open door" policy. Try to be accessible and visible; walk around and show that you care about what is going on. Ask questions and show concern for both the needs of the individual and of the team. Use the coaching process as a road map for both individual and group discussions. Use the principles of coaching in the grievance process and in the discipline process and partnering. Talk openly about the coaching process. Encourage all members of your team or organization to learn coaching skills. Whether we care to admit it, or not, everyone in a group influences each other—so why not encourage the coaching and supportive approach as a matter of course? Literally get up from your chair and make a special trip to find

Coaching is not a "Top Down" tool for just authority figures!

someone you can support without condition, and without the expectation that the conversation has an "ulterior motive." Take a look at your written communications, orientation manual, bulletin boards, memos, and log book entries, etc., to see if the theme of support is strong enough. Then encourage others to be more sensitive to the need to give and receive support.

Gary and Mike — Two Classic Coaches Who Support

Some of the most effective coaches we have seen reach deep to find ways to support their team members. One person, Gary, found that the idea of "undeserved initial support" was successful in breaking through on a difficult situation. It seems that a member of his team was unwilling to accept new changes in technology, and gradually this member's performance began to deteriorate far below acceptable standards. Management instructed Gary to place this person on a formal probation.

Instead of doing this, however, Gary decided to gamble on support and tore up the disciplinary document IN FRONT OF THIS TEAM MEMBER, asking him whether he felt that discipline would help get him back on track. When the other person obviously didn't respect the company's disciplinary process, Gary used this opportunity to simply say, "What does matter to you, and how can I help get us bailed out of this situation?" The team member then began to open up for the first time, sharing that problems at home were carrying over into the work place. The member didn't know how to deal with this and was simply too afraid to ask others for help. By starting a fresh appeal with the team member—based

Gamble on support.

upon support—Gary helped that employee's performance make steady progress. Within six months, the employee once again was a strong and respected member of the group.

Mike is another great example of support being "lived out" in everyday actions. Mike belonged to a member of a group that was the subject of an extensive study of effective leadership behavior which our firm conducted for a Fortune 100 organization. We observed Mike's behavior for several days. We did not interview him, nor did we ask him to fill out a survey questionnaire. We simply watched him, along with others in the study group.

One thing, in particular, that really stood out was Mike's routine when he came to work in the morning. Rather than going directly to his office, as most of us do, he went out into the work area, where he had positive contact with each member of the work group. Some of this interaction was directly "work related" and follow-up from previous discussions. Other moments, however, were spent in casual, caring small talk.

We feel that Mike was saying, "I am easy to talk to. Don't be afraid of me."

People noticed that Mike did not start out his day with phone calls, messages, or meetings. He may even have sacrificed a little of his own time to come in early and make the contact with those already at work. This natural show of support seemed to be a major factor in the high-performance results that Mike achieved. Mike demonstrated a key form of support, and that is flexibility: the ability to shift back and forth between your own tensions, needs, and topics and your partner's concerns, issues, and desires. If you only seek help from others to make life smoother for you, the relationship begins to feel manipulative, one way, or vertical. Flexibility is also the ability to read the situation and give support that reflects the other person's needs or wants.

Too often we give others the support we want, projecting our needs on them. Unfortunately, we delude ourselves into believing that we are being supportive.

These two examples, from literally hundreds of like situations that we are aware of, illustrate the relevant and irreplaceable notion of how support "takes root." We feel that it behooves each of us to place "support" on our frontal lobe and to internalize its application within all groups or organizations to which we belong.

Chapter 8
Step Two: Define
the Topic and Needs

**A problem well-defined is a
problem half-solved.**

The Coach

Chapter 8
Step Two: Define the Topic and Needs

Step Two represents the spirit of openness. Organizations are only as good as the information that goes into them (GIGO—garbage in, garbage out). So it is with coaching. In this phase of the coaching process, you are trying to set the climate for the free flow of information and perceptions. This step is the "discovery" phase of the coaching process. It is about maximizing disclosure and feedback from both partners. The coach—the facilitator of the information exchange—is not a controller, expert, or sole authority in the partnership. The coach must draw out and create a shared or mutual understanding of the situation.

The objective is not to paint the picture for your partner, but to paint the picture together.

Step Two: The "What" of Coaching

With good information out on the table, the two partners can sort through it and work together to create an objective picture of their world.

The initial phases of the coaching model can be described as a process of answering three questions: *WHAT? SO WHAT?* and *NOW WHAT?* Step Two, defining the topic and the needs of the members, is the "What" portion of this sequence. The topic may be an opportunity that can cause good things to happen for the partnership (a "lever" point), or it may be a potential concern that needs to be immediately explored.

If handled in a coaching fashion, this step doesn't need to be emotional, full of anger, and frustration. Rather, it is a "data" step where people try to learn

and understand each other's perspective and mindset. Because of the potential for emotional responses, perceptual data has to be guarded and preserved like a ripe strawberry.

There are two major aspects to this step of the coaching process. First are the topic, subject matter, or agenda: the observation to be explored, the issue, the opportunity, or the concern to be discussed. Second are the critical needs held by both parties: the expectations, goals, priorities, future vision or ideal, or mission. It is useful to know what is important to the other person.

The "topic" is more specific, present, tactical, and focuses on the here and now. The "need" is broad, strategic, idealistic, and visionary.

The need encompasses both a shared and individual stewardship or mission. There may be many topics or incidents to explore, but usually in life, we have only a few truly core needs.

If these two aspects can be discussed in a collaborative way, half the job is done! This step usually takes more time than other steps. In fact, one manager we know of has been spending two years helping to make it clear because she went four years without prior coaching. This step can take more time. This is where you can get a "logjam" of topics, and confusion or frustration can arise as you sort things out. Sometimes, the logjam is about unhealthy "control" of the agenda. Too often, patience and details are sacrificed in the rush to closure. Without question, there will be differences in perceptions.

When pursuing the "What," clarity is more important than speed.

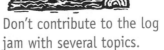

Don't contribute to the log jam with several topics.

The aim here is to achieve a respectful hearing of the topic and needs.

Hopefully, these differences won't frustrate the parties, but will be handled gently, and with the understanding that in all likelihood both coaching parties are partly "right" and partly "wrong." Coaching is based on the philosophy and recognition that we all act on the basis of imperfect knowledge. This step involves a lot of interaction about what is going on and what you want to see going on. Both parties in the coaching process need the time and attention of the other person, in order to express what it is they need.

Seeking Common Ground

Talking things out can create challenges if common ground is lacking. Your associate or companion may have different views from your own. In business situations, the members of the work force may see things differently from people coming from a background of management. An engineer has a different perspective than does a mechanic. Both of these individuals likewise have a decidedly different slant on things than do accountants or administrators.

The key to successfully implementing this step is for both partners to talk and effectively listen.

Expression is more important than agreement. Hear your partner out before you expect to be heard. Stephen Covey says, "Seek to understand before you expect to be understood." Step Two is not a contest to see who is right and who is wrong. Such a contest creates a definite win-lose communication experience. It may be fun if you win, but it can create hostility and unresolved feelings in your partner. Furthermore, the stronger or more powerful person may not have the correct viewpoint.

It is okay to disagree with your partner.

> **Step Two is not about forging an agreement so much as it is about generating data and information to develop a clear picture.**

The only agreement that you are looking for is agreement on the topic or subject area for the discussion. This can be introduced or defined by either party. Still, some consensus on which topic to focus on needs to be reached. You want a mutual understanding, and a mutual airing of perspectives— all without necessarily implying agreement. If, in discussing your partner's position or perspective, or interests, an agreement arises that is natural and genuine, you can, of course, accelerate the coaching process.

 Step Two is really about peeling the information "onion": to look at the presenting topic as well as the deeper, underlying principles and root of it. For example, if someone is submitting inaccurate reports, it may be worth looking at the issue of detail on a larger scale. Is this behavior really about professionalism and commitment to the job? Or is it a simple one-time over sight that can be handled very simply?

The presenting topic is the opportunity at the surface. It is an immediate example, incident, or symptom. By contrast, the underlying topic is the pattern of symptoms, underlying principles, strategies, or fears. It is supported by various incidents and examples.

The presenting topic is possibly one piece of a larger ongoing picture. For example, in one of our popular case studies called Control Systems, a younger, technically trained sales engineer is feeling a bit intimidated by the customer's top management team, and is

The topic of discussion can usually be divided into two parts: the "presenting" topic and the deeper "underlying" topic.

beginning to risk the loss of sales volume by not calling on these powerful personalities. Sales volume with a specific customer is a great topic, but the deeper issue is long-term sales effectiveness: how that is affected by a person's fear of authority, and how the assumptions of others in the organizations can be allowed to shape his/her opinion without first-hand information. We believe it is at least as important to look at these issues as it is to examine how to close on one single sales account today.

> The main goal of Step One is simply to get the conversation to open up, to begin the truth process, to facilitate disclosure and constructive openness.

When some individuals consider Step Two, they may think in very narrow terms. For example, the initial thought may be that Step Two is primarily about giving the persons you are coaching feedback about their behavior. It means that, to be sure, but it also means much more. You can share feedback and impressions, but the main goal of this step is simply to get the conversation to open up, to begin the truth process, to facilitate disclosure and constructive openness. Truth has a power all its own; you just need to keep knocking at the door with a coaching style. Good information can't be suppressed if you are patient and consistent. Giving out feedback is only a tiny part of coaching.

At a deep level, Step Two is designed to create or refresh your insight into the vision, principles, and work that must be performed for your customer. The discussion is never only about two parties; it is also about the third party: the group, organization, or owners who have a stake in the quality of work and in the productivity of the organization.

A coaching discussion should always incorporate the partnership's purpose or mission, as well as each individual's concern or tension.

When you are skillful and patient, you will discover more of the special knowledge and information your partner has than if you try to drive this step too hard, and with too much certainty. From our studies, we have learned that approximately 80% of the time, the person you are talking with is aware of the true nature of the situation. As a friend of ours in the ranching business says, "Don't flog a willing horse." Coaching is the process that enables the other party to open up, and to talk freely and directly. While we all have genuine blind spots, we shouldn't underestimate the possibility that the other person has a lot to share with us, if we can assist in making the discussion mutually useful. All of the data is admissible at this stage of coaching, even the tangential or benign excuses that are ever present.

Generally, we call this approach to coaching "faultless coaching" or "blind coaching." This means that you enter the dialogue in a neutral state of mind, with your judgments, conclusions, or opinions on hold. It means you have elected to set aside your share of emotional baggage and are focused on understanding and learning. The key to "no-fault" coaching is to put the process, not the person, on center stage. Look at the process and flow of events first and the intent and motive second. When you focus on intent and motive, you tend to point a finger of blame. Start by removing you and your partner. Adopt the position of an "observer." Describe the natural pattern of things as a third person. In the example of the young sales person, you might share this thought, "It was true for me and it seems true for a lot of the salespeople who come through our department that we tend to rely on one technique to drive our success, even though each customer and each application is so different. How do you see it?" Or you could say—"If you were to describe your single most effective

> Approximately 80% of the time, the person you are talking with is aware of the true nature of the situation.

technique, what would you pick out? Do you think it is possible to over-use it?"

Be gentle with Step Two—slow down, go easy, take your time.

Try to get in touch with your intuition. Share your thought framework. Try to reveal and label your own assumptions by recognizing and stating them openly. Watch out for prematurely jumping to conclusions and a rush to judge.

Don't assume the worst-case scenario. And don't forget Step One; try to acknowledge the positive intentions that are present. Without Step One, you will come across as cold and distant to your partner. This was a big problem for the manager we mentioned earlier who spent two years on Step Two and totally abandoned Step One, The Support. She tore the support fabric, and today, the employee is better informed, and also very bitter, and is looking for work elsewhere. Try to present the topic more neutrally and less negatively. Then move to the specifics and details. You can be more effective if you will allow yourself to be dispassionate and less accusatory and you won't force your partner into playing the victim role and overwhelming you with defensive excuses. Talk about your impressions, and seek disclosure and honest reactions. This will help prevent an acrimonious discussion of the topic and needs.

Test out your views, assumptions, and generalizations in a provisional way, rather than giving the impression that you are the "keeper of the facts."

The key here is that you don't want to make the people you coach feel totally or terribly wrong. Creating understanding, not deciding who is right or wrong, is the goal.

In Step Three, you can turn the tables around and stimulate reflection. Our maps and filters never quite work perfectly and always need updating. Step Three is like looking at the picture in "3-D," with more depth perception. In Step Two, however, you are simply attempting to open things up, generate some outward exposure, and shed some light on events, choices, patterns, or attitudes. This approach will help create the dialogue you want, rather than a contest, argument, or win-lose competition.

Others will work to create synergy with you if they are not forced to feel like losers.

When you facilitate information sharing in a supportive way, mutual understanding will begin to grow naturally. You can't get to the heart of things if you get in your partner's face.

The Chase Instinct

If Step Two is applied collaboratively, people will see you as less controlling and less manipulative. As a result, they will be prone to share with you the inside information that you will almost always miss if you put on too much pressure, dig too hard, go too fast, or are too abrupt and critical in the data-gathering phase. Sometimes we discover that we are "pushing on an open door," and in the end, we unnecessarily aggravate our partner.

If you enter Step Two driving too hard with a "problem" focus, with a frontal, personal attack, looking to find fault, you will turn the other party off. We call this phenomenon the "chase instinct."

A coach who gives in to the chase instinct tries too hard to pursue either the topic or incidental excuses. Such coaches are not patient: they force issues. Too quick to convince, they don't allow for a more natural evolution of the discussion to occur.

Sometimes, these people are referred to as "pacesetters." Setting a pace is not necessarily bad, although it can get in the way of dealing with the real issues. The issue is knowing when to push, and when to pull—when and how to draw out the different perspectives on the data. The chase instinct can also be a problem in Steps Four and Six, the plan and the excuses. Ideas can be pushed too hard and too fast. Likewise, people can succumb to the hideous process of playing "fetch" with excuses, and not call the game when it has turned into manipulation. More will be said about this in later chapters.

Don't play "fetch" with excuses.

The chase instinct is also part of the discussion we will have on direct and less-direct methods of coaching. Over the years, it has been an eye opener for us to see how quickly we can move to the offensive mindset, form an opinion on limited or one-sided data, and then become the advocate, the expert. We can even unknowingly mount an attack and then wonder why our companions, or partners, are defensive.

Remember, it is impossible to "un-ring" a bell. Once you raise the defensive walls, it will take considerable effort and time before your partner relaxes and opens up.

People are prone to form quick opinions and then to begin nipping away at the heels of others. This is often true for either or both members of the coaching dialogue. You also see this phenomenon occurring when any significant event happens in society and the media report on it with only preliminary or partial coverage of the story while it is "hot." Don't allow yourself to fall into this trap.

Our experience suggests that you not always insist on serving up the topic yourself. Facilitate! Unless your coaching partners have true "blind spots," help them identify and clarify the topic. Use a consultative approach, look for the opportunity, and then reference the expectations and vision the partnership is trying to create. The following suggested dialogue may assist you in this quest: *Help me understand your strategy. I could be assuming the wrong thing here. Let me run this by you. If you don't see the decision maker, how will we get the signature on this account?*

Within the coaching concept, we call this general process of moving from the broad to the specific as "going through the funnel." You begin with the general and non-personal, and then work in mutual ways to distill the specific issue that the two of you together feel is critical to examine. The coaching process will help "boil off" the marginal stuff and get you to the meaty part without inflicting wounds to the tender areas or vital organs of the relationship. Then, if your partner is unable to see important things going on, or if the urgency of the situation requires swift and decisive action—you may need to set the pace and lead out. However, the "lower press" approach makes it more acceptable to be direct and set the pace when you have to.

> **Just as if you were looking at any picture, you need to look at the whole AS WELL AS the details in order to really get a correct perspective of it.**

This is part of the very central concept of *balance*. A key goal in coaching is to size things up accurately and honestly. It doesn't work very well if you are like one of our learners, who said, *"Don't confuse me with the facts. I already have an opinion."*

As a coach, you serve as a primer, or an "igniter." You simply strike up the conversation around the topic at hand, the other person takes off a little, and you guide the discussion through the funnel. You can sit back and listen, understand, and try to identify the really key topic, or the deeper and more important underlying issue or principle. Generally, the people you are coaching will gradually open up. They will subtly tell you where they can use some support, input, or ideas. All of this means that you are at the wide end of the funnel. Gradually, you can help sort out and focus on the "main area of attention."

Remember that coaching is a little like the focus ring on a camera; if you try to focus on two real topics at the same time, they will both be blurry.

There are many facets to the discussion. You need to help others get all the perspectives—the long and the short view—if you are to create synergy. Try to remember that some people like to cut to the chase, while some have a low capacity or slower topic digestive system. You must use some flexibility and judgment. Don't always do what you want to do. Instead, consider other's styles as well, and generate a good mix. Share with them your desire to proceed slowly, or to move fast, as you talk about the subject matter. Reach a decision with your partner on what should be addressed, and help bring it into focus.

Elaborate, Define, and "Empty Out"

Suffice it to say, the first job in Step Two is to elaborate, define, and have each person "empty out." The rule is: Diverge before you converge. If it is a simple issue that has surfaced before, it is okay if you go right to the point. If it has been a while since the issue was discussed, or if the personalities are fragile, draw a long funnel and proceed slowly. In either case, you need clarity and honesty. You don't want either ambiguity or defensiveness.

As you move deeper into the issue, test the waters more with honest and assertive observations. Disclose your own perceptions, vulnerabilities, and contributions to the issue. Coaching topics and issues have a short "shelf life" before they become too historical, so try to seize the moment and engage others, no matter how easy or difficult.

Concentrate on the here-and-now. You can't reshape the past. You can only shape the future.

If you truly WORK at understanding and listening to the perspectives, views, and data people give you, you can create the conditions for synergy, for a helping relationship, for people to voluntarily give up their energies and talents for the group or the community.

Working at understanding their views of the situation doesn't mean that you must give in, accept, or abdicate your data, your experience, or your opinions.

As you move through Steps Three and Four, differences will become less significant and less divisive. In fact, these very differences may be the material and the catalyst for new, productive, and creative solutions. Just try to get an objective handle on the nature of the situation.

Keep Step Two simple and as un-emotional as possible.

In Step Three, you can begin to exercise the mental perspective, the paradigms, the beliefs, and the mindset that are necessary to create alignment. Don't make the mistake of jumping from Step Two to Step Four with a "solution focus." Step Three will create the positive, creative tension, introspection, and reflection necessary for people to decide that they want to "plan" with you.

Don't Sink the Coaching Ship

When you think of this step, think about raising only as much dust as you can settle.

Step Two can work very well for you if you focus the discussion on the "here-and-now," rather than on the past. It was pointed out in our earlier book, *The Coach,* and is worth reiterating now, that becoming too historical in your coaching perspective, or referring to missed opportunities or mistakes, can be the fatal flaw that will sink your coaching ship. For example, systematic annual performance reviews provide an opportunity to look at a broad time span; the coaching perspective is more on today and the near future. Systematic appraisal systems work poorly when coaching is sparse. It is difficult, if not impossible, to recover from the "black hole" of coaching when you are addressing unresolved topics from the past—water already under the bridge. It is essential that you keep a strict limit on the number of issues to be explored. It is best to limit the discussion to one or two at most. Approach the topics one at a time, and complete the coaching process as far as possible on each issue before tackling the next and strive for understanding without blame.

As one client so aptly stated: We are not trying to solve the issue of world hunger in our conversation. Coaching topics need to be bracketed so that any one coaching opportunity doesn't try to ramble over a lot of diverse topics. If multiple topics emerge, say that you are willing to schedule as much time as necessary, as soon as necessary, to give them full and fair attention.

It is important that you focus on the tangible and the more observable, and less on the subjective nature of the topic. Be cautious that you don't identify the main topic as the intentions, character, motives, and personality of your partner. If you unintentionally or unknowingly attack these core features of the person, you may encounter defensiveness and excuses that will block the understanding you are trying to achieve. It may be a hint that you are making the topic too personal and focusing too abruptly on the abilities of the person you are coaching.

When you discover what to talk about with someone, you may have discovered only the visible edges— what we earlier called the *presenting topic* or *issue*. Deeper facets, principles, or an underlying core may be important to get at.

If you tend to allow critical incidents to drive your coaching episodes and remain reactive, you may be missing the real opportunity to be proactive.

> **Observable surface events, opportunities, or incidents provide the catalyst for meeting. Use these as a springboard for the more central, strategic, or core issues.**

Your objective is to begin the truth process by helping create an accurate picture of both the presenting and the underlying topics. Whenever a group of people come together to achieve a common objective, there will be many levels and angles to explore. Try to keep the discussion focused on responsibility, not so much on fault or causes. Express the point that the "causes" have multiple sources: The system/environment is often at fault as much as any individual. Coaching is probably more about fixing processes than about fixing each other. Don't try to fix intentions, character, and motives. If these are out of alignment, coaching is not the solution. You simply may not have the core building blocks for a partnership in the first place.

If you are coaching on a difficult topic, try to look for the opportunity that accompanies every problem. Seek out the lessons and insights that can be gained and applied in terms of future expectations, needs, and direction. You will gain an entirely different spin on coaching as you explore the agenda from the perspective of the glass being "half full, rather than half empty." Seek out the silver lining before you discard or ignore a problem. Pursuing this approach is more gratifying and creates a lot less defensiveness.

In addition to establishing the subject matter, topic, or issue, the parties in the coaching process need to explore their overall needs and wants. This provides the context and backdrop for the immediate topic at hand. A particular topic or issue will frequently serve as the impetus to meet and talk. Even so, it is the needs, visions, expectations, and hopes that create a more complete discussion and dialogue picture. The needs and hopes should come from the heart. They are deep and meaningful.

Define the Desired Reality

Your needs and motives explain what is important to you, as well as what you are trying to do. If you listen and ask questions, you can likewise learn about your partners' intentions, motives, and needs. So Step Two is clearly designed to look at the need, the "desired reality," or where you want to be.

Step Three, on the other hand (although closely related), looks at the possible gap between current reality and desired reality in the hope that new energy and urgency will be created to develop Step Four's plan of action. We all will have some blind spots. We just need an equal amount of maturity to locate and own up to them. This step requires an ability to be "in touch" with your needs and goals so that growth opportunities can be realized.

By exploring needs and wants, parties in the coaching dialogue can find common ground upon which to fuel the plan.

Successful coaching requires that you explore both parties' perspectives. Since perceptions are nine-tenths of the law, you will want to be careful not to force your view and your opinions. You will likewise want to be careful not to exercise your formal or moral authority, or to revert to command-and-control tactics. Truth is in the eye of the beholder.

The Chinese leader Deng Xiaoping once said it this way: "Try to gather all the facts so that you can discover the truth."

In the end, Step Two is about truth and honesty, but it is not about brutal and punishing honesty. It is about gentle honesty. The intent of Step Two is to achieve a fair understanding and a shared "felt need" for change.

As mentioned earlier, it is unfortunate that some people use honesty and openness as a warrant or excuse to be blunt, hurtful, or cross. Active listening and a two-way exchange facilitate the understanding and sharing of observations and perceptions. Carl Rogers' first of three conditions for change is "Accurate Empathy": skillful, reflective listening that clarifies and amplifies the other person's own experience and meaning (1959, p. 5). The ability to describe physical events and data in a natural way will help lower resistance, denial, defensiveness, and avoidance.

Realize that there will be some tension—hopefully good tension—when your presumptions meet the other person's excuses and resistance.

This approach won't eliminate these reactions, but it *will* minimize them to some degree. If defensiveness is allowed to congeal, it becomes more difficult when Step Three tries to dissolve or crack the rigid paradigms. Facing reality is difficult enough without having someone pressing down on you. The coaching process paints the picture in such a way that the two of you can sort out facts, truth, and learning. You each have control of your beliefs, yet you cannot be the captain of Step Two. You must be willing to be a passenger along the journey.

Sharing Your Interpretations

Try to describe and share your interpretations, as well as your group's expectations. Outline the vision of the entire group; then clarify your coaching partner's part in realizing that vision. Ask your partner to describe both the highlights and the challenges that are faced. Invite your partner to describe the "pluses" as well as the "minuses." One of our clients said, *"Look, I am not good at fairy tales, so just give me the ending."* This degree of abruptness is likely to turn off the openness!

Allow the expectations, along with the requirements and standards that are independent of your individual wishes and personal interests, to carry a heavy load. By doing this, you don't necessarily have to play the "heavy" and impose your will on another person. Let the expectations impose a special will. After the other person reacts and discloses his or her views, offer yours. Use descriptive language, and "own" your own views. Taking responsibility for your own views helps reinforce constructive openness.

Begin with impressions, rather than with certainties.

Here are four examples from actual conversations:

1. *"Perhaps it is just me, but I often have the feeling that our suppliers are not clear on the details that appear on the work orders. I know that at times, I personally become confused when I read them."*

2. *"I have been wondering if the way we currently process the re-work items will fit the company's needs to keep pace with the competition."*

3. *"I am trying to envision how the customer will see these new changes with the amount of information now in their hands."*

4. *"What kind of numbers would you like to see for our department in the next four months? What kinds of changes will it take to help get us there?"*

Sometimes if you can create a vivid picture or illustration in the other person's mind, it will help to solidify what you have been thinking about. Remember that you can be honest and direct without attacking the person you are coaching.

The following style will be interpreted as a personal attack: "Why didn't you get that paperwork completed?" You could depersonalize this a little by saying, "What are some of your thoughts and experiences with the planning sheet? How is the paperwork going for you? Is it something you feel comfortable with? Do you see the role it plays?"

By using this approach, you are building a platform from which you can stage deeper non-threatening inquiry. When you start from a natural and neutral perspective, you say to your partner, "You haven't taken a position to this point." This approach will allow your partner to be more open and creative, and to build more ownership and empowerment around the issue and the plan.

> **The truth doesn't need to be unnecessarily painful, critical, or judgmental. It just needs to be open and honest.**

Empathic Responding

Some other things that can help are to ask before you tell, watch your level of certainty, and avoid getting into the role of advocate too soon. You need to create enough time and space for the information to flow and be metabolized by you and your partner. Don't try to judge the information. Instead, listen and examine it from the other person's perspective. This process is called "empathic responding." It involves learning to place yourself in the shoes of the other person, and to respond from that position.

Allow the information sharing to diverge, dump it out, and vent your emotions. Don't allow the initial excuses and explanations to sidetrack the direction of the collaboration.

> **Guard against taking the excuses personally. Excuses are normal and harmless human reactions. In fact, these excuses can tip you off to the amount of fear, anxiety, and frustration the other person is experiencing in exploring the topic.**

We are not suggesting that you need to give in, or to agree with the excuse. What we *are* saying, however, is that you simply need to actively listen, and to look at the other person's perspective, learning what he or she is trying to communicate to you. You need to offer reassurance, and to test your interpretation of the excuses. You do this by stating and reflecting the excuses back to the other person.

As we alluded to earlier, you won't find a right and a wrong, as all people are some of both. You can simply provide some tactful dialogue and leadership, then inquire as much as you advocate. How you view the topic will depend a great deal on where you have been, what you have experienced, your mindset, your needs, and your fears.

> **Inquire as Much as You Advocate**

> **When it looks as if you are headed into a conflict, try to clarify that your intention is to not say the other person is wrong. To the contrary, state that you simply see the issue differently and that you have another "take" on it.**

At that point, try to redirect the other person to the core needs, expectations, and requirements. It is okay to respectfully disagree and still keep the coaching process moving. As pointed out by Fisher and Urry in their book, *Getting to Yes*, try to define the parties' "interests" rather than concentrating on the "position" or opening argument. "Interests" is just another way of saying needs, desires, or a vision of "where you want to be in the future." Search for

Focus on Shared Stewardship

the common ground of needs, which are broad and more rational. Positions are more emotional. The position is one specific "end" point. There is no room for creative options. Become a servant of your shared needs and the mission of your team. Ask your partner about their stewardship, talk about your stewardship, and focus on shared stewardship. Address both human needs and task needs. Both parties need to answer this question: What are the binding needs for our work and for our personal well-being? These needs are ultimately the glue that binds the partnership.

During Step Two, you don't need to worry about agreement or consensus. Convergence will begin to occur in Steps Three and Four.

The main thing you must do now is to find out the other person's perspective. If the parties in the coaching process understand and know the expectations, vision, aims, and goals, they have a very good chance of achieving alignment and synergy in Steps Three and Four. If you create some trust and openness at this stage, the reflection and agreement will emerge. You just need to help each other through your blind spots, fear of vulnerability, and defensiveness.

Chapter 9
Step Three:
Establish Impact

ESTABLISHING IMPACT is the lubricant for the slow-moving gears of change. It is a vital transitional step in moving from the issue to the forward-looking steps of action and commitment.

The Coach

Chapter 9
Step Three: Establish Impact

Step Three epitomizes the spirit of exploration and insight. It is the step where constructive tension and discovery come together to form the springboard for mutual agreement and positive change. Step Two deals with the more tangible, obvious, or empirical. Step Three is more slippery. It deals with our blind spots, things we have forgotten or taken for granted. Step Two was the WHAT? stage. This step is the SO WHAT? stage, in which a shift in thinking about the topic of the coaching dialogue occurs. In this process, a "readiness for change" element comes into focus that creates the motivation to talk, explore, and think more deeply than before. Once two partners have defined the current reality and the desired direction, you can begin to examine and ponder the gap if it exists. In a sense, Step Two deals with the admissibility of the data and Step Three looks at the weight or impact of it.

Step Three is about discovery —checking reality and waking up the mind.

Galileo once said, "You cannot teach a man anything. You can only help him find it within himself."

This statement captures the essence of this vital step. The coaching process helps others internalize the need to do something different. Some people in the sports community recognize talented players because they have a gift to see the "whole court or field." Your partners need to see more of the field so they can arrive at decisions about new options and new behaviors. They don't need you to spring a plan of your own making on them. If you do, the planning and commitment steps are a lot harder. After the mind is focused, you can then help bring out the actions, agreements, and strategies that fit the situation.

Once the parties have agreed to open up their minds—and whatever preconceptions they may have had about their situation—they create the constructive reflection needed to sustain new paradigms and beliefs.

A more open mind allows us to reconnect with our feelings about a particular topic that may be covered up over time or with daily routines.

Make special effort not to hurt your partners or to exercise their volatile emotions. The intent is not to paralyze them with guilt, remorse, or sorrow. The concept here is more like allowing or enabling them to unfreeze their mindsets. In a way, the impact appeals to something deep within, like sensibility, interests, integrity, and ethics. A metaphor for this step is a lubricant that helps tranquilize resistance, conflict, and denial. You can't always see this lubricant at work, but it is there, and it makes a difference. The hope of Step Three is to enable discovery without creating animosity or resentment.

Coaching is not about punishment. It is about flexibility, openness, and vulnerability. The impact should create a healthy and creative tension as the coach helps the two parties look, discover, and realize the need to examine traditional things in new ways. Because perspectives can become rigid and brittle, and because any topic has multiple sides (some of which may not be easy to see from any given angle), a process is needed to help rotate, or turn the topic.

The coach's role is to help facilitate this discovery, to help both parties see outside their own individual boxes—and to even physically move outside of the boxes of their comfort zones in order to experience fresh views of the topic. This creates the motivation to share, to open up and continue the dialogue.

Examining the Forest as a Whole

When you truly experience the other side, you can create the common ground necessary to move forward.

This step is like the forest and the trees. In Step Two, the forest and the species of trees, including their size, features, and details, are defined. However, if you became too detailed and too myopic, you lose sight of just where you are standing.

Step Three helps you look at the forest as a whole, and to understand the relationships between the trees, the environment, and the forest's functional effectiveness. We have heard some people refer to this step as the "geometry" step because we are exploring various angles. Within this step, you are stepping back from your actions, cleaning your perspective lens, and seeing the picture in "three dimensions" so that you can better make decisions and act upon them. Allow yourself to be surprised.

Think of this step as a way of disturbing or gently agitating complacency.

More effective plans can be designed when both parties know more about each other's thought process and the mental models that subtly guide their behaviors.

The agitating process in Step Three makes the topic more interesting and relevant. It creates the motivational leverage for growth, learning, positive change and improvement. Ultimately, impact is the difference between intent and results. It is designed to bring the coaching parties to take more responsibility for the way they think about the topic and any changes that may be appropriate.

Once the effects and ramifications of the situation become clear, both parties are closer to being ready to make changes that will be true and lasting.

In Step Three, people come to better understand their relationship to the topic. They can get in touch with the gap between intent and effect. Then sensitivity about the need and awareness of the topic are heightened. This step applies to generating interest in positive changes, as well as problematic situations. A key part of this step is to heighten interest in the opportunity or problem before you go to the drawing board of action planning.

There are constant lessons to be learned, and insights to be gained if you will simply step back and examine the situation. You can reassess your real goals, priorities, beliefs, and assumptions. This, in turn, will help create convergence of viewpoints like nothing else we have seen—that is, if the parties are willing to be open to the impact and to the facilitating efforts of each other.

If you are engaged in true, positive coaching, the impact process should strengthen, refresh, and reassure. It should also provide the "front end" motivation to engage in new and creative strategies. If coaching involves problems and difficult situations, this step will help the parties discover the "disconnect" or misalignment between what they are doing on the one hand, and what they would like to do on the other.

Once the parties perceive the dissonance, or incongruity, they can begin to square their actions and choices in Step Four, the plan. The fresh appreciation, sensitivity, renewal, awareness, or realization that comes through this step helps you "jump start" into new patterns of thinking and relating. Education professionals have called this the "teachable moment." All partners must work at building their ability to tolerate and to accept that they constantly need to refit their views and perceptions to match new realities and needs. Everyone has a personal and moral responsibility to discover the truth. Step Three puts the parties on the threshold of true change and cooperation.

The Teachable Moment

While Step Three can do a lot to create common ground and generate agreement, it is frequently avoided or neglected altogether.

> **For many reasons, people don't allow their experiences and viewpoints to teach them. They close themselves off to the "pain" associated with change, getting their egos wrapped into the picture, and locking out fresh viewpoints. They don't let their experiences counsel them**

The coaching in Step Three rests on the idea that when the student is ready the teacher will appear.

Step Three may not be as tangible as some of the other steps. It is designed to create positive interest, emotional excitement, a sense of urgency, and a positive pull that doesn't come from the power of consequences or outside forces. Yet the "chase instinct" is often allowed to draw people prematurely into the plan. You must guard against indifference, complacency or a rush to a solution in order to achieve reflective openness, or impact.

Step Three is an important step, and it can be an enjoyable step if you don't expect an instant dawning, awareness, or miracle. It can make you feel as though you are simply planting the seed of an idea, but a seed that doesn't sprout instantly. An important mental process must unfold between Step Two (the topic, data, exchange of information, and feedback) and Step Four (the plan, action, goal, pay dirt, and end zone).

Only on rare occasions do people experience "sudden impact." More often, it will hit you gently and in less dramatic ways.

To change metaphors, it may help to consider what happens when an ice cube melts. The frozen cube can be like the way people sometimes look at a topic—set and rigid. It is like their current view of the world. To change the shape of the cube of ice, you must put it  through a gradual melting process, into a more pliable state. In the liquid, more flexible state, you can reshape the cube into a form that will meet your needs.

The transition from the original set state to the more flexible, and thus more moldable state, is achieved by establishing the impact. It is similar to unfreezing the ice cube. Crushing the ice cube destroys the structure and does not allow it to be reshaped. The ice cube must be warmed up gently—not by taking a blow-torch to it. The coach is the catalyst, or "prompt," to induce this melting process.

Try to be patient and create a little space and silence in order for your partner to "tune into" these feelings. You cannot force or rush the process. You must allow the parties to meditate on the impact. This can be the start of a compelling and emotional transformation in thinking. As you begin to examine issues from this perspective, you can generate the positive tension that requires some resolution. The tension doesn't have to

Silence is one of the most under-utilized communication tools. Words alone will not awaken the super-consciousness.

be harsh. You want to create a soft, almost vicarious collision with reality. The hope here is that a closer examination of the situation will allow more of the facts, reality, and truth to surface.

Unfortunately, many human beings have a too-well-developed ability to rationalize, form opinions and beliefs, and stick to traditional positions. This is sometimes referred to as "cocooning."

The impact provides the "bed of motivation" to start something happening, to stop something, or to encourage things to continue as they are.

Some of us find that a reality check is too uncomfortable. Perceptions and assumptions have a powerful effect on actions and attitudes. Few things in life can be clearly and factually seen by only one person. The power of coaching comes from the fact that two or more people are working to validate the facts and the picture. In our coaching model, we color Step Three *red* to signify its warming aspect. The red color means that the parties need to stop and allow the impact to soak in.

Opening Belief Windows

Step Three disturbs comfort zones of the mind by cracking open "belief windows." If you are successful in causing re-examination, introspection, consciousness raising, or of disruption of complacency with the status quo, then the chance that both parties will entertain the possibility of serious voluntary change increases dramatically!

If people are stirred to contemplate the alignment of goals versus methods within their own minds, the chance of seeing fresh action flow out of the interaction increases. The decision to act occurs when you finally acknowledge that your point of view is at odds with the needs of the current reality and that excuses and rationalization can't offset the tension. If the other parties are only riding your coattail of readiness and raised consciousness, then they will either resist change, or they will comply with only token effort. If you don't create relevance and significance, you won't create the internal motivation required for lasting change. You may only create the skin-deep motivation to comply while your partner is watching.

> ### A real "Ah-ha"

It is difficult to change behavior if you don't change paradigms and viewpoints. Impact means that you have in some way gone to work on the topic. It means you have arrived at a shared conclusion that current behavior is not leading in the direction that the partners want to go. It means you now have true ownership for the situation.

Enormous strength and leverage emerges when individuals recognize their own blind spots. It is a real "Ah ha!" moment.

Receptivity for collaboration, and innovation then increases dramatically. The experience of seeing the gap or of gaining a different perspective on thoughts and actions versus desired goals, expectations, and needs can be very powerful and moving.

As people see this gap, they are usually motivated to consider and then make appropriate mid-course corrections. If, as coach, you can facilitate this change in perspective, you can accomplish significant long-term change. If you can help others see new pictures, or see that life is dynamic and moving, and that it requires constant change, you can help generate interest and motivation at a deep level.

As a word of caution: you need to carefully judge how "shocking" the new, dynamically produced picture should be.

With Step 3, you are trying to create a significant emotional "thought" rather than a significant emotional "crash." There should be enough shock to create attention and caring for the topic, but a radical shift in focus is rarely achieved overnight. It is usually an evolutionary process, taking time to digest and contemplate. If you have your coaching partner's full attention, you are in a position to explore new options. You have created a bridge between the topic and the action plan. Even so, if you overdo it or try to punish your partner with the impact, you will undoubtedly create ill feelings that will set the course of action back.

A Dynamic File System for Change

Perhaps this would be a good moment to pause and share the experience of a colleague. While he was in graduate school pursuing an advanced degree, one of his professors gave the class the assignment to create an entirely new "file system" for the things they were learning. The professor then explained that most people keep "static" file systems; that is, they insert information into folders over their lifetimes, and allow these papers and ideas to have found a permanent home with no thought of ever extracting them and throwing them away.

This type of file system, the professor explained, becomes not only cumbersome but, in time, weighted down with non-essential and outdated materials. In turn, the owner of the system utilizes its contents less and less as time passes. The professor then went on to say that from that day forward, the students should develop "dynamic" file systems—regularly examining the contents, adding to and taking from them as they desired.

So it is with implementing a "dynamic" approach to change in our lives. It is a healthy, proactive *modis operandi* for the group— especially when done in a positive, caring way.

An Explosion of Energy

As coach, you must remember that you cannot control this process; you can only help and facilitate.

It is truly exciting when the impact ultimately kicks in! There is a strong, positive pull to act as the impact light bulbs turn on! Issues then come into greater focus, and a whole new world opens up within the minds of the coaching partners.

Impact is like a mental explosion, and the coaching process can play a vital role in igniting this explosion. The coach can provide some tools or help to light the fuse, while helping to keep the powder dry. The coach 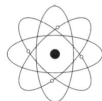 can also suggest a target for the cannon, although it is ultimately up to the other person to get excited and explode into action, creativity, and thought. Ultimately, they must hit their own targets.

As coach, you can help sponsor, encourage, and enlighten so that a decision about change can be made. You can help bring interest and attention to the topic and need.

We don't want to make it sound as though impact is an event. It is rarely a "one-time" shot, and it is never completely "finished."

Rather, it is more of a continuing evolution with regularly experienced "highs" and "lows."

An issue can come quickly into focus, yet without frequent coaching, it can just as easily go out of focus. At times it is easy for others to see the impact, while other times, it becomes so challenging that it seems impossible. But even if the other party becomes a reluctant participant, the coach can proactively share

No pain, no change

experiences and stories to help the partner achieve an open mind. A little pain or agony is sometimes created. Thomas Edison seemed to be his own coaching partner as he developed the light bulb. Thank goodness he kept going and learning, even after so many apparent failures and frustrations! Remember the "no pain, no gain" saying? In coaching we could say "no pain, no change."

In order for change to take place, the power of the impact and awareness must outweigh the resistance to change.

Successful change or improvement takes dogged dedication, a great deal of work, and tremendous concentration. Even when change becomes painful, you must resist the temptation to remain in your "comfortable rut." Keep climbing out onto the ground of progress. The impact must be stronger than the forces reinforcing current choices and behaviors. The impact may require time to germinate, develop, and mature. Patience, then, becomes the first order of consideration. There will be exceptions to this guideline. However, some of our partners may need to hit bottom and "dry out." A soft landing of the impact may not work. We need the support element in place so they don't crash and burn.

It is extremely easy to try to make a gigantic jump from Step Two's "TOPIC" to Step Four's "PLAN," while totally missing the contribution of "THE IMPACT" to the coaching process. Actually, it may become necessary to make the impact the first part of the plan and to create a real impactful, growing experience if you are not succeeding in communicating the impact.

"Landing" the Impact

It is a real bonus if the impact "sticks" on the first pass. Effective partners know how to use the coaching process and how to "land" the impact just like the prize trout you've dreamed about hooking and landing. Yet, when the person on the end of the communication line feels the impact "hook" sink in, it is normal and natural to resist and struggle. A lack of self-reflection carried to an extreme can develop into a serious character flaw that will lead to difficult relationships.

People are capable of being their own best coach, as well as their own worst enemy, when it comes to helping themselves out of difficulty or into an existing new opportunity. It takes maturity to be willing to re-examine, to look at a side of a situation that may not naturally appeal to you. People are generally taught to defend their existing beliefs, operating ground rules, and values. The impact may be painful, however, and we hesitate to engage in painful activities. Too much impact too fast can create resistance.

> Some people have a real inner fear of examining their operating principles and what they are really trying to accomplish.

The key point is this: THE IMPACT IS NOT A CRUNCH OR DISASTER! It *is* the early warning that can give you the insight to a problem or opportunity. But you can't sit back, rest, and assume that all you have to do is what you did in the past. Someone once said that the definition of insanity is continuing to do the same thing and expecting a different result. A whole range or spectrum of impact levels begins at one end with a deep and real blind spot. Along the spectrum arc phases of complacency, arousal, surprise, awareness, awakening, interest disturbance, shock, pain, sorrow, guilt, shame, and hopelessness. The key is to achieve "balance" along this continuum.

> "If we do what we always did, will we get what we always got?"

Don't overkill this step and create more irrationality. What is desired is that new light be created that will guide the way to some excitement and improvement.

You don't need to be overly aggressive in helping others see the gap, the "disconnect," or the global perspective. Just be there—be consistent, supportive, and caring. Others won't look at the light you can share unless the support and trust is intact.

Knowing Your Partner

"Establishing" impact is different from "telling" impact.

To establish impact, you must know your partner's motives, values, and goals. What will impact you is different from what will impact your partner. To ask your partner to think about the impact of his or her current attitudes and behavior on others is only valid if the "others" are a critical value. A critical shift may be required in how you go about it: Think about impact relative to your partner's values, motives, and goals, not yours.

We are often reminded of this shift in perspective during coaching discussions with children. Their blank stares when we offer our sage advice or recommendations are a result of our perceiving the situation and discussing it from our values—not from what is important to them. Until we reorient the situation relative to what they are trying to achieve or be, there will be no "felt need" or impact.

A Beautiful Example of Impact

Helping someone see the impact can be very simple. One of our friends shared an elegant example of how his spouse compassionately conveyed impact. Our friend, Bob, has a love affair with fast, imported sports cars. He likes to drive them and he likes to drive them fast and push the engineering limits of these vehicles. On one occasion, Bob was out on a short trip with his spouse and youngest daughter riding in the back seat. As soon as Bob got behind the steering wheel his "Parnelli Jones" paradigm started to settle in. With Bob's driving gloves on, he started through the gears, and then, once he hit the thoroughfare, his speed began to accelerate. He didn't say a word to his passengers, he just enjoyed the pure exhilaration of being in control. Bob was in his element. He was having fun, because for him, driving was a sport. It was a test to see how well he could dart in and out of traffic. In his mind, he was on the Indiana Speedway. After a few minutes, his wife had the good sense to gently put her hand on his shoulder and very quietly express the following words: "Bob, your daughter is watching you very carefully right now." Bob's daughter did not hear those words. She was beginning to enjoy the thrill of the sport. Just like Bob, her mind was caught up. She was only fourteen years old, two years away from receiving her drivers license and having the opportunity to take the wheel like her father. Bob shared with us that the words of his partner resonated in his mind for weeks. Nothing else needed to be said. These words created the introspection and thoughts about the behavior and attitudes that he was inadvertently passing on to someone he valued. We have always been impressed with this story and how effective, short, and illustrative the impact can be if it is done well.

What Do We Gain From the Impact?

If you are able to help turn the topic around, upside down, if you can prick the consciousness and throw light onto potentially outdated concepts and practices, you will grease the skids for the plan of action, decisions, strategies, attitudes, and new ideas. With Step Three, you want to create good, creative tension or friction. Just like cholesterol, there is good tension, healthy tension, and there is negative tension. The purpose of this step is not to beat your partner up or mug them with reality. Rather, it is to keep a balance while not escaping reality. The hope is that this step will empower, refresh, and renew the spirit, and not cause people to feel bad, to experience guilt, or to become embarrassed that they haven't seen or felt the impact on their own.

Without impact, interest, and felt need, you risk creating shallow plans and dispassionate agreements.

The great hope of Step Three is that the partners in the coaching process will gain a broader understanding of the main topic. Hopefully, the partners will discover how their mental maps and interpretation filters color their views and perspectives. By learning more about their maps and tunnel vision, they can discover facets of the topic that are true and accurate. They can then discover facets of their behavior that can be candidates for change.

The simple fact is that each party in coaching is partly right and partly wrong, and that all parties should be open to re-mapping. Every viewpoint has flaws and strengths. The objective is to avoid a crash of two points of view, because of course each of them has some validity. If the partners can step outside their boxes and get in the frame of mind of an independent third party, then they can make progress. This process of introspection is called "spectatoring."

Each partner needs to ask the other what a third party would suggest, or simply how a third party would view the situation. Sometimes, seeking out the viewpoint of other key stakeholders, or even viewing the situation from the perspective of a competitor, can be a real eye-opener. Coaches must work and be open to the fact that through healthy, two-way communication, the impact will begin to affect them. Their eyes will be opened, and their flexibility will be enhanced.

Step Three is simply trying to gain a commitment from both parties to look at the whole.

It is a simple fact that a coach can't share light if that coach doesn't have light to share. If the coach is closed and resistant to being enlightened by the other partner (which resistance, by the way, may stem from a sense of being insecure), then both parties, as well as the task, will suffer.

When both parties catch the vision, the impact will work a very natural process. When the impact is forced, however, and people are *made* to look, they won't see the same thing as the coach sees.

If the coach has to drag things out, or pull the coaching partner along, it becomes an uncomfortable and laborious experience for both partners. Remember that the ears and the creative mind won't work if the eyes are closed.

The Insightful Coaching Lens

Some situations are simply not coaching situations; some people truly suffer from a condition of "impact deficit disorder."

Think about it for a minute, "the eye cannot see itself without a mirror." In coaching, the coach serves as this mirror. Your partners can help the process if they open their eyes and see that perhaps the price of continuing down the same path is greater than the price of change. If the coaching mirror is not there to avert impact, it is less likely that the coaching process will stir up the motivation for change. Instead, conflict will erupt into a full blown perception war.

Value Analysis

The coach can go about helping increase the felt need for change in various ways. One approach is to do a *value analysis* on the status quo. In a sense, you are costing out the pluses and minuses on proceeding with the current approach. This works quite well when both tangible and intangible benefits and losses are involved. This will help both partners relate more closely to the issue and will "bring it home" by personalizing it more. If, after doing a value analysis on the topic, it appears that change is not appropriate, then both parties can feel confident that the right thing is being done—based on the best available knowledge.

A Role-Reversal Technique

Another effective approach is to go through a legitimate *role reversal* process. A role reversal simply means that the coach and the other person envision the mindset and perspective of someone else. For example, the two of you can share impressions and feelings from the customer's perspective, from that of another department, from the community, from the shareholders, or other stakeholders. Don't forget to switch places with the person you are coaching and vice versa. Our experience suggests that sometimes the role reversal is uncomfortable for both parties. In fact, it should be uncomfortable—that's what makes it work! Therefore, people may have the tendency to slip out of the role about as fast as it is created. Don't get upset. Just hang in there, and help reset the stage to reverse the roles again and again.

Often, looking through the eyes of others opens up your own.

Other Techniques

There are times when the sharing of examples, case studies, and anecdotes can be effective—if they are not shared to excess, and sharing is done with taste. In fact, if the illustration exposes some of your own vulnerability, it will send a sincere message. In essence, the other person may have an impactful experience if they can vicariously encounter the topic and impact. You can also use metaphors or generalizations to make connections which increase your grip on the topic.

Effective use of legitimate and genuine questions can help people magnify interest that is dormant or hidden. You might ask probing or penetrating questions such as the following:

- *What would we accomplish if everyone on the team used the same approach that we have been using?*

- *We are each looking at this from our own perspectives. What are the other viewpoints that we should consider?*

- *How much are others struggling with this issue?*

- *How fair are we being to people other than ourselves?*

- *Are we meeting established goals and expectations?*

- *Are we getting what we really need out of this situation?*

- *Is the current situation meeting our core human needs?*

If the questions don't work, try some honest "I" statements. For example: *I think the customers will feel they are not getting full service. If I were in the shoes of the other department, I might feel uneasy about this new idea. Let's talk about the angles we are looking from. Let's look at this from some more angles.*

These statements will help prevent paradigm paralysis.

In the world of sports, coaches have team members look at the game films (the big screen in full color). The visual picture is self-explanatory. The pictures are big and clear, and there is no escaping reality. Some people need a very vivid game film. Or, even more! Others must actually taste it, see it, hear it, or smell it. Their physical senses may require hard impact in order to believe that there is value in considering change and growth.

An Arousing Alarm

If your coaching partners can look over the horizon by using Step Three, they can see the opportunities and the potential for change. In Step Three, you are creating the desire or reason to become interested and focused. Unfortunately, at times people choose to "hit the snooze button" when life's alarm goes off. They don't get out of the box; their perceptions and paradigms are eclipsing reality. The power of this concept came through to us one night while staying at a hotel that was experiencing some problems with its fire alarm system. For some unexplained reason, false alarms went off about every 20 to 30 minutes all night long! At first, the alarms had our attention, and we would respond to them in good faith. It didn't take long, however, before we grew insensitive to the alarms and began to ignore the signals. In effect, we became "impact blind." Subconsciously the mindset developed that we would only take the alarms seriously if we had stronger signals and could smell or see smoke. That would become our new threshold of impact that would then lead to action.

Somehow, it finally dawned on us that this was a very dumb set of guidelines, and that the price of action was really less than the cost of no action—especially if the "real" alarm went off. So we took the precaution of evacuating each time the alarm went off, even though it was terribly inconvenient. Ultimately, it is your choice. You decide what to attend to.

You can chose to factor in the signals or rationalize them away. In a way, the coach is trying to be a credible and valid signal.

Two pairs of eyes are better than one.

Sometimes, the best warning systems are inaccurate, and that is the reason the two of you need to jointly look at the signals and the alarms that are out there for you. Together, you can avoid a lot of "paradigm paralysis" or other forms of self-absorption.

Serious change does not occur until there is introspection and greater light and awareness.

Step Three creates joint ownership so that both parties can feel proprietary about the situation. They feel that they "own" the situation and can take responsibility for it. Both parties need to make choices and decide together what to focus on. Even so, if both parties can shift their perceptions, they can have a much greater range of future choices.

As a coach, you can't control another person's consciousness, beliefs, or choices. Society and competitive pressure won't allow you to divert so much effort on control procedures, and frankly, you can't afford to exert it.

Your job is only to help enlighten. Plato once said that the unexamined life is not worth living. He, perhaps better than anyone else, understood the true nature of impact.

Remember that patience, a little silence and space, and the use of good questions will help condition and exercise perceptions and paradigms. It is difficult and really unnecessary to predict how and when the impact will sink in. For some, the impact may occur if the pinch is felt in a very personal way. For others, this may be less relevant. Instead, it may be that what is really important is how this affects significant others, whether they be co-workers, friends, or family.

For some, it may be impact at a more global level, and the affect their behavior is having on many.

> **Human beings are all different. Different things capture their interest, raise their awareness, and stir them to new thoughts, feelings, and actions. So it is with Step Three. The things that impact individuals (cause their minds to focus, think, and reach resolution) will vary depending on the personality.**

There is no set formula that we know of. But having some knowledge of the people around you, and having thought about what excites them and what their passions and hot buttons are, will guide you as you search for the appropriate impact.

The principle of impact is well illustrated in the following true story. At 9:30 on a July evening in 1988, a disastrous explosion and fire occurred on an oil-drilling platform in the North Sea off the coast of Scotland. One hundred and sixty-six crew members and two rescuers lost their lives in the worst catastrophe in the 25-year history of the North Sea oil exploration. One of the sixty-three crew members who survived was a Superintendent on a rig, Andy Mochan. From his hospital bed, he told of being awakened by the explosion and alarms. He ran from his quarters to the platform edge and jumped 15 stories from the platform to the water. Because of the water's temperature, he knew he could live a maximum of only 20 minutes if he were not rescued. Also, oil had surfaced and ignited. Yet, Andy jumped 150 feet in the middle of the night into an ocean of burning oil and debris.

When asked why he took that potentially fatal leap, he did not hesitate. He said, "It was either jump or fry." He chose possible death over certain death.

The underlying belief is that as we think, so shall we act. This is clearly illustrated by James Allen in his book, *As A Man Thinketh.* Some of the environmental awareness posters have a great photograph of the earth from outer space, with a caption that reads THINK GLOBALLY AND ACT LOCALLY. Impact sometimes seems like the story about the elephant and the blind men. They all made different assumptions about their reality, based on which part of the elephant they happened to be standing near. If individuals are not cautious and open, their perceptions will create their own prison. Experiences need to be shared to get a handle on reality and learn how to cope with challenges. In some ways, this captures the essence of Step Three. It sometimes feels like being in a box, with the escape instructions on the outside. By working jointly at locating and acquiring the instruction, the escape can be accomplished.

No one person can be absolutely certain about anything.

Helping others look at the less visible, more subconscious, and perhaps distasteful side of a topic requires work, time, and courage. Remember that with this step, you don't want to become aggressive. It must work on its own. Don't try to hang the other person out to dry. Tough and insensitive communications may "churn and burn" the relationship. You just want to warm up the thinking of both parties to consider changes and ideas.

So what is the basic form and structure of impact? What are the types of pathways to greater consciousness or super-consciousness? How do you arouse the mind? How do you shift the mindset or alter the focus of your current thought process? Unless you can project, transcend, and reflect, there will be no deep and abiding change within yourself or within others. People will be thinking and doing things because they were told to, not because they believe it or can see it on their own.

The "Role" Factor

We mentioned this briefly already, but it deserves a little elaboration. "Role" means: the position, assignment, task, or function that you are in. Naturally, many people have a narrow view of roles, thinking about self to a far greater degree than we think about others. This is not to say that self-interest is bad. It is just that if it gets carried to an extreme, you end up hurting yourself as well as others.

We all want to be successful at what we do, but if you over-focus on your own success, you may be undermining it without realizing it.

If you can reverse roles, shift positions, and hold on long enough to really experience the emotion and capture a piece of the vision or world as others see it, you can be a more effective partner and team player. If you can't make this shift, you may be killing the cooperation, interdependence, and synergy that make the partnership work.

The "Need" Factor

The second facet of impact is "need." This refers to your own goals, as well as the goals of those with whom you are coaching. This is where Step Two and Step Three link up. As you examine your current choices and attitudes in the context of your guiding goals and values, you may find inconsistency and incongruence. With the help of others, you may be

A self-inflicted shot to the foot

able to see an alternate picture. In fact, you may find that your patterns of behavior are flying in the face of where you really want to go.

It may surprise you how often you can be "off track," despite being clear about where you want to end up.

Sometimes there is a complete disconnect between the path you are traveling and the destination you want to achieve. Sometimes you need to stop long enough to check the roadway and account for the activity and the effort.

Activity and effort can be totally unrelated to the goal or end that you have in mind. We are reminded of the old airline joke where the captain came on the intercom and said, "I have some good news and some bad news. First the good news. I am happy to report that we have favorable head winds and that we're making very good time. Now for the bad news. We're lost!"

There are times that you can help others, and be helped by them, in clarifying and "checking in" to see if one's efforts and one's needs are reasonably synchronized.

Once again, the Maslow Hierarchy of Needs is a useful framework in terms of levels and types of human needs and motives. For example, many people find that they enjoy and strive for security, yet, ironically, do things that do not support this objective. Failing to see the links or the system that is at work, you may be inadvertently hurting or fighting those around you who help insure our security.

The "Time" Factor

The third facet of impact is "time." If you shift the time focus and hypothetically roll the clock forward, you can push the relevance buttons and brush the rust off of your rigid perspectives. For example, you might ask:

- *If we stay with the status quo and don't change, or adapt to the pressures and demands of the business, in what condition will we find ourselves two, five, or ten years out?*

- *How likely are things to be the same as they are today?*

> **Five-Year Plan**

There are times when people get stuck in the "time warp" of the past, present, or future. Balance in time thinking is vital to success. If you are stuck in the present, and don't factor in what time will do when you don't update, re-tool, and stay abreast, you can adversely affect your own performance, as well as the performance of those around you. If you are always anticipating, hoping, and wishing you were in the future, you may discover that you are missing some quality opportunities right now. If we live in the afterglow of past memories, you can handicap your relationships by running out of energy and not finding the meaning of the future and a way to contribute.

The "Size" Factor

The fourth facet of impact is "size," the intensity and distance of your experience. For example, you may be unaware of whether our behavior would yield results that would be good for the group as a whole. Productive behavior patterns can lead to distant and abstract payoffs. Likewise, counterproductive behavior sometimes has distant implications. You can help create impact around a subject if you are able to **magnify** the issue so that it is clear, present, and vivid. This makes the subject more exciting. If gaps or disconnections exist, the parties can then design a responsible and appropriate plan or agreement. The impact is designed to bring the parties to that decision. The impact can also be created when you reduce, simplify, and cut through to the essence of the issue.

Step Three is designed to help focus or refocus on the truth and the reality.

 # The "Location" Factor

The fifth facet of impact is "location." If you can help others visualize the subject from another vantage point, you can harness more power. This, in a physical sense, could be a significant shift. In other words, you may want to place the participants in the coaching process in another location, department, or place. Then, from this perspective, you can entertain some interpretations and conclusions for future courses of action.

Encourage reading, training, and developmental activities.

On a broader scale, effective coaches encourage people to rotate assignments and advocate job flexibility so that people don't get into thinking and skill ruts. Invite members of your group to meetings, have them talk to the customers, and encourage them to participate in benchmarking projects. If it is possible, have them observe competitors; teach them how the organization makes a profit, manages its resources, or is in some other way held accountable for creating service or value.

The heightened awareness or impact may kick in gradually, or it may kick in suddenly. Sometimes it feels tedious and long-term as you plant the "impact" seeds. Sometimes it is gratifying when you see some immediate response and interest. The bottom line is that no one can control the weather. Likewise, no one can control when the impact will blossom. If coaching is possible, it is because the parties have worked to achieve an open mind. We believe the mind is a lot like a parachute. In order for the parachute to function properly, it must be open—and so it is in coaching with others. The parties need to strive for open and receptive minds. To become better at the things you do, you cannot skip over the discovery step.

As a partner, you have the responsibility to create as much truth and understanding as possible, even at the risk of some pain.

Chapter 10
Step Four: Initiate a Plan

Using others' knowledge of the situation, as well as his or her creativity and talent to establish a workable plan, will help insure success.

<u>The Coach</u>

Chapter 10
Step Four: Initiate a Plan

Step Four, initiating an action plan, captures the spirit of synergy and collaboration. This step symbolizes energy, the future, and a readiness for action! Some of our clients describe this step as the "R" step, which stands for *responsibility*. During this step, the coaching partners become serious about the decisions and the division of labor.

This "working" step involves deciding who is going to do what, where, when, and how. It is sometimes referred to as the "pay dirt" step of coaching.

Planning—Where the Rubber Meets the Road

In gold mining terms, "pay dirt" means high value, richness, a place to invest effort. This is what the previous steps have been leading toward. For example, Step Three, the impact phase, helps the parties decide whether a plan, change, or agreement is a good idea. Step Four is where "the rubber meets the road" and decisions are made as to what the change or agreement will look like. It is the step where concrete plans are made, and where the strategy is set in place to score real points for each member, as well as for the team as a whole. This is the step where the partnership can make a contribution to the community, or where it can move forward. A plan in a coaching context is not simply behaviors and actions. It is also an agreement, decision, or understanding that will help guide the work and learning that goes on in the relationship.

Sometimes we describe Step Four as the "brain" part of coaching, the more intellectual and cerebral part of the process. It is a more rational and systematic thinking part, as well. Many people who think in traditional terms do well with some aspects of this step. They recognize the natural part that thinking proactively, identifying options, and envisioning the steps play in the accomplishment of important and challenging goals.

Still, for a body to function at all, there also needs to be a heart. Some would argue that the heart is more important than the brain, but such a debate is immaterial. To have a chance at survival and any kind of a life-style, you must have both. For this reason, Step Five, the commitment phase, is separate from Step Four, the plan. You must be strong and effective in creating the strategy and ability, as well as strong in creating the will and the desire.

The key to unleashing synergy in Step Four is to manage creativity, brainstorming, and risk taking. Differences in interests or needs, as well as in solutions, positions, and plans, are merged into collaborative solutions. Both synergistic parties require maintaining an open mind, becoming participative, and sharing ideas.

To achieve a state of collaboration with the other person, you must create ownership and work jointly to come up with a solution. Some people don't like joint ventures, preferring to go solo. People can't be expected to hop on board automatically, but a little bit at a time. Generally, people who are engaged in coaching tend to commit and carry through on the things that they have helped create.

Both members need to see themselves as contributors to the planning and decision-making process—not as the ultimate authority.

Because both partners need to be involved in the solution design phase, they need to relax their control needs and passion to be "the experts." This isn't easy for those who have high control needs or like vertical relationships.

You might say that coaches are valiant advocates, but not advocates of specific pet solutions. Coaches act as catalysts for the development of an agreement that contains all the prerequisites of a good plan. As strong advocates of the collaborative process, coaches believe that two heads are better than one.

Good partners try to avoid "preformed" or premature solutions.

Collaborating or co-opting the plan with other people is so important because if *you* try to say it and create it for others, they will forget it. Conversely, whenever you direct the plan, you inadvertently set yourself up as the expert, and potentially as the scapegoat, if things don't work out well. It is tempting for others to say, "I tried to tell you" or "I told you so." In contrast, when your plan is right on target, you inadvertently reinforce a sense of helplessness and dependency in others. It also destroys the support and generates resentment. It is tempting for others to feel like you have all the good ideas. In today's environment, more empowerment and fewer feelings of inadequacy are needed to make good things happen.

If *they* say it and create it, they will believe it and "own" it.

In some respects, Step Four is where you create real value for the organization. This is where you have the opportunity to capitalize on your creativity and on the lessons learned from the current situation. If the impact of Step Three is beginning to work, you will see some initial signs as you and your partner become involved with the plan. The desire to plan, develop, and grow are key team assets if people stick with and trust the synergistic coaching process.

Within this step, there is a wide range of styles or flexibility choices that can be made, depending on the situation or circumstance. Some of the style choices and some rules of thumb will help guide your selection.

A Continuum of Choices

Try to envision a continuum with various points along it representing your style choices. At one end of the continuum, Point 1, you can create or share with your coaching partner a great deal of freedom and discretion in handling the plan, as well as in coming up with an appropriate course of action. The rationale for selecting this style is that the other person is competent, mature, knowledgeable, willing to learn, or a self starter. As such, these people should be empowered and encouraged to decide.

Point
1

You might also select this style if your partner is a subject matter expert in the technical aspects of the plan and you are not as gifted in that field. If the complexity, uniqueness, or newness of the situation renders both of you novices, this coaching style might provide some good development experiences for your partner as they figure out a viable solution independent of help from others. Finally, this may be a good style when ample time and other resources permit trying out and experimenting with novel approaches.

Point 2 on the continuum is where your style is one of sharing input and ideas. Brainstorming, or helping with the brainstorming process, is greatly needed. By participating, you help guide others through a positive decision-making sequence until a plan emerges that meets the requirements of the situation. You might select this style if resources and time are

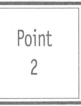

Point
2

available to work through this approach, and if it is important for your partner to own the agreement and believe that it is the right thing to do.

If your partner will be working independently and voluntarily on the plan, acceptance, as well as a high level of comfort, is needed. If the situation is challenging to both parties, you will want to tap into the synergy that can result from this style. This very supportive style enables people to build self-confidence and feel worthwhile.

Point
3

At Point 3 on the continuum of styles, you attempt to design the plan and become more of an expert. You generally build a precise solution, but you are open to new possibilities. Then you clearly explain it or teach your partner how to do it. Doing this allows questions and discussion, but not a lot of modification.

If the person you are working with is struggling to see the impact or relevance, this approach may fit. If your partner's personal needs, expectations, and motives are out of alignment with the group, or if your partner lacks experience, then you may need to take a more influential role in Step Four. Still, you must remember that with this approach you reduce the amount of leverage available to you—simply because your advocacy and "certainty" could cause some resistance. Resources may not be used as effectively as when there is more participation, ownership, and "buy-in" from your other coaching partner.

Point
4

At Point 4 on the coaching style continuum, you are at the extreme of command and control. For example, you can issue specific, step-by-step instructions; give others your plan; and then, without discussion, tell them what to do. This style is hardly coaching; it is telling, but you *could* resort to this approach in an extreme situation or crisis, when there is no time left to interact.

This extreme approach is obviously dangerous: you are clearly reinforcing a strong dependency relationship by teaching the other party to rely on the coach's brain, to live with being only a robot. A dangerous warning sign is when the other person repeatedly asks, "What do you want me to do." Sometimes this is appropriate; more often, it is a cop-out. Your partner is not accepting or taking real responsibility. You may be one of the reasons. Point 4 can foster this to the detriment of everyone. Even though it is a possible measure, in the long run, it is certainly unsatisfying for most people. It creates a *vertical* relationship, which is most uncomfortable, especially for the one being controlled.

Over use of "command and control" feels pushy and creates fear.

Using this approach is almost like spanking a child as a form of punishment. Child psychologists tell us that when a parent is controlling and regularly spanks a child, this form of punishment does not "extinguish" the child's inappropriate behavior. Rather, it becomes a negative stimulus to the child, and the child will continue to "act out" and resent the "abuse" that begins to be heaped upon him or her. However, on rare occasions, to make a clear impression—or to accomplish a specific learning moment— an appropriate spanking can be healthy and constructive for a young child. One example might be when a toddler wanders into the street and the parent needs to let that child know how truly dangerous the street can be.

**You may get by with some of this
authoritativeness—if it doesn't become
your customary style, and if you don't use up your
bank account of support and credibility. Just don't
allow it to become so routine that it blossoms into a
negative reinforcer for those on the receiving end.**

Control and
coercion can
become an
addicting way
to relate to
others because
of a temporary
but counterpro-
ductive feeling
of power.

Learn to rely on
respect, com-
munication, and
dialogue to
achieve under-
standing and
consensus.

The key objective, then, is to help the change process
"get off the dime." Generally, the more your partners
are in the dark, the more you may need to tactfully
and caringly move along the continuum toward Point
4. But, the more your partners know, feel confident,
and committed, the less you need to play a high-
profile role in this step. Point 4 causes your partners
to become lethargic and lulls them into a false sense
of security. It creates an immunity to learning in your
partner. Reserve the more abrupt and potent forms of
interaction for genuine emergencies where you have
little to lose, and where the advantages of taking
control of the plan offset the long-term disadvantages
of defensiveness, apathy, and resentment.

The objectives of this step can become a little confusing—we fully realize that. On the one hand, Step Four
is about creating "deliverables," while on the other
hand it is about balancing involvement and contribution from both parties. If you can focus on the "ends"
(a common goal), and if the other person is willing to
help figure out the "means" (the methods and tactics
used), you will create a powerful alliance. Ultimately,
this will lead to a productive and stimulating long-
term relationship that will continually change and
improve.

Begin the planning process with the desired result as the guiding light. A common goal, not the personalities of the two players, should be the primary driver. Let go of pre-established ideas about how the plan "should" work. In the plan, it is okay to stretch, to encourage both parties to go beyond their perceived limits—IF THIS IS DONE WITH COMPASSION. You can encourage and challenge others until they reach the limit of their safety zone. Then, your job is to help others see the risks and overcome them. Don't stop giving them material and moral support during the process and be willing to accept some false starts as the plan gets up and running.

Three Types of Plans—The Action Line

As you enroll people in the planning process, take advantage of the three types of plans that can be created. **First** is the typical, immediate, forward-looking plan that right away helps put the partnership on a proactive course of change. This type of plan doesn't have to be large. Size is not critical. It is simply important to get the engine started. Later, after things are set in motion, you can become ambitious and elaborate. As in golf, "You don't have to kill the ball!" Start where you have a reasonable chance of making some initial headway.

The **second** type of plan is one that takes a step back (to Step Three) in the coaching process. If you are still having differences and conflicts, you may need to create a plan that will focus on *clarifying the impact.* For example, you may want to help the people that you are coaching conduct a formal or informal survey of their customers, spend a few hours or days rotating jobs, or even take a temporary assignment with a different team. Encourage your coaching partners to check-in with others, and be willing to do the same when it comes to getting outside of your own box. Ask them what plans or activities they can devise to help shed some new light on the situation. These types of plans are expressly designed to set the stage for insight and motivation that will ultimately produce a more substantial plan.

We have personally experienced situations where we had to adopt a **third** type of plan, one that requires the two coaching parties to stay put, to dig in deep, and to work at designing a rich, full solution, decision, or agreement. In other words, the plan is to "make a plan!" Some situations are complex and involved enough that you need to think them through carefully, conduct some research, or allow enough time for the creative juices to begin flowing. This process may require some time, and it isn't worth doing a quick, "knee-jerk" reaction until all of the options have been carefully thought through. With this type of plan, you don't want to take a "ready, fire (oops), aim" approach!

Using the Action Line—Be Realistic

You will be more successful using the coaching mode if the plan matches the situation and the individual that you are engaged with. Most of us would like to see the change process start out fast, in "high gear." We have repeatedly indicated that coaching requires patience, and so it is with this step. Rather than creating a plan of radical change, hoping that the two of you can reach consensus on some long-term agreements, it may be more reasonable to begin at a moderate point on the

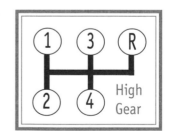

"action line." An action line is a series of choices, from very broad and general on one end, to very specific and finite on the other.

▶ **The first point** on the "action line" deals with especially sensitive or controversial situations. The plan may be for the two of you to talk more about the topic and listen to each other more. This keeps the dialogue open and helps you cope with defensiveness and hostility.

▶ **The next point** on the action line might include the parties considering the impact and the views of the other person, without the expectation of coming to terms with any specific action plan.

▶ **The third point** on the action line might be the creating of some initial plans, or even trial baloons. The ideas here are *not* to create a full-scale plan of attack but, rather, to test out some ideas on a pilot scale. These kinds of plans are safer, less risky, and less frightening, but they allow both partners to test out new behaviors and ways of thinking.

▶ **The final point** in the action line is where serious, full-scale changes are proposed, and action is taken. Significant and ongoing commitment is required for major adjustments in behaviors, beliefs, and values.

Recommendations for Success

Several specific recommendations may help you achieve greater success in establishing a plan. First, be two-dimensional in your thinking. That is, what is the situation or topic trying to teach you that will be helpful in the future? What are you learning? When you encounter this situation again, what could or would you do differently? What could you encourage, prevent, start, or stop to achieve more of what you need? How will you act or think in the future? These are long-term strategic plans. They work on the root issue.

As a second recommendation, ask what you can do now to achieve an immediate solution. These answers constitute short-term strategic plans. These might include interim actions that deal with symptoms as well. It is easy to become too futuristic with your plans, to overlook opportunities and needs that exist right now that are right "under your nose." The plan should include something for both partners to do that is concrete from both a long-term or strategic aspect, and from a short-term tactical focus.

You will be able to create more success with this step if both parties are willing to cast off preconceived ideas, solutions, or pet options. You need to be willing to challenge conventional thinking. Synergistic coaching works if people start fresh, don't play the role of the expert, and don't try to be the hero with all the answers. You will need to coach yourself and the other party to think openly before you jump into the middle of this step.

Learning to Let Go

Learning to "let go" of pet solutions and control can be a very challenging aspect of Step Four. Try to avoid entering the dialogue with pre-existing ideas, solutions, or emotions. A key to initiating a plan is to not manipulate each other or try to get the other person to think and do what you had planned on doing ahead of time. In a sense, you must go into this step with an "empty agenda." Your real agenda is to contribute positively to the process of creating a good plan. Think of Step Four as an evolution. First, start with **initial** ideas from each party. Second, try to facilitate new or **emerging** synergistic ideas. Third, consider **merging** ideas. Fourth, try to settle on some **final** ideas. Focus on facilitating, not on playing a heavy role or forcing your favorite choice. Ask your partner this question: "What do you think we should do now?" Then, after asking, listen carefully to the response.

Final Ideas
Merging Ideas
Emerging Ideas
Initial Ideas

A reminder of this is used in our workshop. Before the practice sessions, we ask the coach to write out their favored solutions, to fold these papers and put them in their pockets, and to carry out the discussion without reference to your favored solution.

Gently "diverge." Try to explore by asking, "What do we need or want to have happen? What are the common interests, aspirations, goals, results, and objectives that we want to achieve? What resources and constraints do we need to work within? Is there flexibility in the constraints?"

Einstein once said, "Keep it as simple as possible, but no simpler."

At this point, you invent and brainstorm options. After asking, "What options may exist?" close in on something that is sustainable. Judgment and balanced thinking are critical. Create a "flight plan," flow chart the strategy, mentally rehearse the process. Help your partner see that you are facilitating an agreement and not controlling it. Empower this person with support, reassurance, adequate flexibility, and resources to become an activist for the plan.

There are times when you must recognize and trust the strengths and differences that other people bring to the party. It won't work to try to bring them around to your way of thinking in an artificially nice or sweet way. In coaching, the real goal is to create synergy and to maximize the power of two minds working together on one topic or issue.

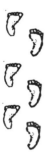

Don't be afraid to think "small" until you have tested the waters. Don't over plan the plan. Pick out some "tiny baby steps" at first; be cautious about trying to solve the whole problem at once. Instead, try to draw out others' ideas; then examine your own tolerance level for risk, and exercise a level of flexibility that is consistent with the situation. People will have a higher sense of personal responsibility if they have true ownership and involvement in the action plan.

Try to create space so the other party has enough playing field to experiment and practice.

Sometimes it helps to share your understanding of the boundaries. We call this "chalking the field," which means helping to provide a framework and developing absolute limits with the other person. Help figure out the means and methods to achieve the results that are necessary to meet the requirements and boundaries of the situation.

A key part of coaching here is to encourage the expansion of response options, to stimulate choices, and to help create possibilities.

Helping to Decide

The next phase is to assist with the decision-making process. Decision making is more logical and rational, while the brainstorming of ideas is more intuitive and spontaneous. There are many effective strategies for decision making, and most approaches have some good, common-sense basics. Here is a simple framework that has worked really well for us over the years. First, define the goals, results, or outcomes that you want the plan to achieve, as well as the resources available to work with. Then brainstorm and compare the options that the two parties have created to the list of goals and resources that are available. Calculate how well each option performs against the goals and the available resources.

Resist the temptation to jump at the first attractive option. Instead, subject your final strategies to a test of any potential obstacles or negative consequences that may make the apparent number-one choice unacceptable.

A good plan is one that is constructed with the thought in mind that some changes and modifications will be required before the two parties arrive at the final destination.

Make sure your partner understands that you are willing and available to talk openly and make any changes that become necessary.

In Summary

First, expectations of both parties need to be expressed. There should be target objectives, and the resources for executing the plan should be mapped out. Plans should be specific, measurable, achievable, realistic, and time bound. Some people call this boundary leadership.

Second, you should then generate alternatives and give your partner the flexibility to challenge conventional wisdom, as well as to push the boundaries. See if the plan includes some growth and development opportunities for both parties. Both individuals need to be open to learning and experimentation to the degree possible.

Third, as coach, make every effort to create some initial success. Disclose and open up on what you are and are not willing to risk. Keep in mind, however, that real failure begins only when the two parties have agreed to stop trying. Watch out for blind determination to make a poor plan work. Someone once told us that when you are in a hole, you should stop digging. That makes perfect sense, although sometimes the tendency with a bad plan is to just dig faster! Make an initial plan that will move the project all the way to its completion. Don't settle for a concept or idea when something concrete is needed.

Remember that a good plan that is not clearly outlined or documented is only a WISH in your mind!

And so we ask the big question: *WHAT IS THERE TO LOOK FORWARD TO IN INITIATING A PLAN?* To answer, you are first setting up success for the next step, which is commitment. Secondly, you are building the stage for synergy, as well as for breakthroughs. Third, we are setting the stage for ownership and for greater interest and motivation to make the improvements and changes a reality. Fourth, you are trying to reinforce the concept that synergistic coaching is not a command and control style of relationships, nor is it an autocratic, authoritarian, or expert-driven relationship. Rather, it is a *consultative process* that values input to help drive better action plans and commitment.

Chapter 11
Step Five: Get a Commitment

This step is designed to "lock in" a commitment to try.

The Coach

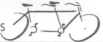

Chapter 11
Step Five:
Get a Commitment

Step Five reveals the spirit of conviction and owner-ship. Commitment is a verbal signature to the plan. It is aimed at building integrity and testing for resolve. The primary thrust of this step is to discover the initial commitment level, to build on it, and to create enthu-siasm.

In a sense, commitment is more than cooperation. It is a feeling from deep inside that you are "enrolled" and loyal to the plan. Commitment needs to be honest, open, and candid.

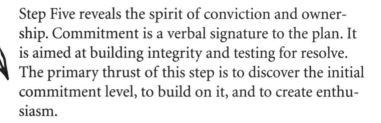

Step Four, the plan, repre-sents the brain power, while Step Five represents the will power.

Lying at the heart of the coaching process, commitment is designed to stir up excite-ment about possibilities and potential. While Step Four deals with strategies and tactics, Step Five focuses on willingness and confidence to implement the plan. The plan is logical, rational, and tangible in nature; commitment is emotional and more psycho-logical in nature. Joining the head and the heart will, in turn, create a successful coaching experience.

There are two kinds of commitment: A relationship commitment reflects a willingness to work with the other person. Commitment to the outcome requires the willingness to work on a plan of action, which involves specific, tangible actions, and behaviors.

Step Four, the plan, focuses on what can be done. Step Five, on the other hand, looks at what individuals will do. A good plan necessarily costs something. The currency that pays for it is your personal desire and integrity. If partnerships are to be productive, then integrity and a healthy sense of obligation need to exist.

Coaching functions under the principle that commitment is more important than dreaming or intellectualizing about the plan. If the plan doesn't pass the commitment phase, then coaching isn't complete. More interaction and effort are required.

The true test of coaching effectiveness occurs when you petition and others develop interest in applying the action plan or agreement. If things are going well, it should be easy to discover the commitment. If, however, there are obstacles in the relationship, the discussion, or the plan, then evidence of resistance, hesitation, or objection will begin to rise to the surface of the dialogue. You will feel yourself working harder and feeling more frustrated when this happens.

Voluntary commitment represents the heartbeat of coaching.

The key to voluntary commitment is to facilitate and guide the discussion of commitment. With this step, you are trying to learn what is wholly possible and what is improbable. The most productive way to learn about your partner's commitment is to ask the direct question. Are you confident? There is an amazing effect on your coaching partner when you lay it on the line in a simple non-abrasive way. It gets your attention. It makes you think and focus.

The Depth and Power of Commitment

Step Five has more depth than initially meets the eye. At first glance, getting a commitment may appear to be a mechanical procedure: venturing out and asking a single question. Make your own resolve and commitment clear; then call for the commitment of your partner. As a coaching partner, your role is to encourage, empower, and inspire the others: to "light their fires" and motivate them into action. You cannot burn the fire or force the plan, nor can you make the commitment for someone else.

The key is for you, as coach, to bring some excitement and enthusiasm to the discussion, and to let the other parties know of your confidence in them—to assure them that you recognize their importance in the ultimate success of the plan.

In this step, you need clarity about integrity and accountability. It doesn't matter how much you collaborate on a plan, or how much you share and give feedback; if integrity and accountability are lacking, you won't go very far.

In order to bring closure to this step, one of the most important questions you can ask is, "What can each of us do to the plan, or to our relationship, that will enhance commitment?" This is a nice tie-in to the next step, which deals with resistance and excuses that need to be discussed and confronted openly, yet with great compassion.

Once you have exercised your thoughts and questions about commitment, make every effort to step back and give your partners space; allow them to "choose" their level of commitment.

Without commitment, nothing else works.

You can likewise tap into Step Seven and explore some of the natural consequences and outcomes to help shore up the commitment level.

If the commitment is cloudy, you need to do what is necessary to clarify and strengthen it—even if this includes scaling back on the action planned in Step Four in exchange for a higher level of commitment. This commitment must be true and straight; it cannot be one wherein you vector, or where you are indirect or obtuse.

This step implies that if there is a will, there is a way, and that it is almost impossible to stop a committed will.

In Step Four you are trying to find the way; now in Step Five, you need to try to find the will. Keep in mind that if commitment hasn't been verbalized, it hasn't taken place in the mind. Questions that work well for us in clarifying commitments include:

Run the numbers and see how it adds up.

- *Can you do it?*
- *Will you do it?*
- *Can you give it a try?*

These types of questions address whether the other party is able, knowledgeable, and equipped. Will you do it… reveals whether your partner sees value or senses that it is the right thing to do. Ask people on a 10-point scale how strongly they feel about the solution. This helps make the commitment more visible and open. You move beyond mere cooperation and can test the quality of the coaching work that has been done in the steps leading up to this one. If you don't get a pretty high number, you have got to do some more "polishing" on this step.

Levels of Commitment

Step Five is truly a test of where you are in the coaching process.

We have found that in today's relationships, real commitment is at times a rare commodity. While high levels of commitment are a worthy objective, that may not always be possible to achieve at the beginning of the coaching process. It may be more important for both parties to be "aware" of commitment levels, and to be sensitive and realistic about what to expect—as well as to be knowledgeable about where the parties are now—so that people are not hurt or disappointed later on.

Real, lasting, and deep commitment does take time to solidify and is not going to appear overnight. Just as the farmer must plant seeds and water them, as well as allow the warmth of the sun's rays to "do their thing," so, too, must you, as coach, plant, nourish, and provide the supporting "rays" to your partner. Developing this mindset is a very satisfying process and sets a coach-minded person up for repeated success—not only in the present coaching relationship, but in all facets of life.

We have identified and labeled six levels of commitment that are easy to recognize. Some of these commitment levels require nothing more of us than moving aside and not becoming an obstacle to their natural commitment. Other levels need to be developed and enhanced.

Activist

A high level of commitment is very easy to define. A highly committed person is an "activist"—someone who wants the plan or agreement to succeed. Activists will do whatever is required to make things happen: taking risks, stretching, pushing, testing structures and constraints in order to "pull it off." They talk to others about their commitment and want their associates to support their level of enthusiasm. They are excited and enthusiastic, and they promote what they want to have happen.

> **6 Levels of Commitment**
> 1. Activist
> 2. Enrolled
> 3. Sponsor
> 4. Actor
> 5. Resistor
> 6. Rebel

With all of the energy created by activists, it is possible for them to become carried away and ultimately go overboard. When the pendulum swings too far, the activist may lose focus and become estranged from members of the group. We have an associate who served in the Army. While on a dangerous assignment, he became friends with another soldier who, in fear of losing his life, had almost overnight "found religion." Others were initially happy for him because he was happy. This supportive energy from the other soldiers began to wane almost immediately, however, this soldier became such an obnoxious zealot that he was almost unbearable to be around. In fact, he became so zealous that he was given a mental evaluation and was then transferred. He had gone "over the edge," so to speak, and was finally given a medical discharge from the service. All of this resulted from a good person not being able to balance a high level of commitment with behavior that was acceptable to the sensibilities of the group.

Although the above example is an extreme case, it does illustrate the challenge of becoming an appropriately committed activist, while not turning others "off" with excessive enthusiasm. The key, then, is to develop this activist mentality at a measured pace so that the positive energy and commitment can create a synergistic increase in enthusiasm among the other members of the group.

Enrolled

People who are enrolled are advocates to a degree. They want to achieve the plan, and they work very hard to see that this is accomplished. However, they may not take as many risks as the activist, not wishing to test the limitations and constraints in the environment. They will work within the framework, but they may do so in a quieter fashion. They will likely be less vocal, allowing their actions to speak for their commitment, but will work diligently to achieve a high level of performance. In short, they will be low-profile champions.

Sponsor

Sponsors are supportive; they accept the challenge of the task, and they can visualize the benefits of doing so. Basically, they do what is expected. They can be counted on and are almost always considered "good soldiers." They may not spend a lot of extra time and energy on accomplishing the task, but they meet basic expectations and are valued by the group.

Actor

Actors go through the motions and make it appear as though they support the plan. Still, deep inside, there is a sort of grudging compliance or state of apathy. For some reason, actors have not worked through all of the issues that lead to higher, more fulfilling levels of commitment. A degree of "approach-avoidance" behavior, a form of mental restriction, is still apparent.

Ofttimes, the actor, or drone, will give "lip service" to the task, but real action and commitment are not yet firmly established. The effective coach can have a great impact on these people by proceeding slowly, and with a gentle, caring attitude.

Resistor

Resistors don't test; they don't even want to try. Something is holding them back—perhaps apathy, a lack of interest, low energy, lack of rewards, or even a fear of failure. Perhaps their plates are overloaded, and they can't tell the difference between urgent and important priorities. Sometimes it is part of their personality; they may be critical, negative, or skeptical by nature. They likely won't work on the plan at first, and they may take the position that no one can make them do it.

These people may not be willing to examine the benefits, to explore, or to take risks. They use excuses like fear, habits, time pressures, other people, or simply the impossibility of the situation. These individuals are sometimes caught up in a "victim" mentality. They feel things are working against them, and that there is a conspiracy out there. This attitude leads to a state of confusion, anger, and frustration, which may actually cause them to "hold the plan hostage," as they work against its success. The coach will need a "full court press" to be of much help to these people.

Rebel

These are people who have no commitment or interest in seeing that the plan succeeds and may, in fact, work contrary to the consensus of the group. If they are to be retained as members of the group, rebels will need the help of everyone. They may need assignments that don't jeopardize the basic mission of the group. The rebel may have a real stake in this role or label. The rebel has a very clear and strong identity. They may be proud of this identity and want to protect and uphold it.

The Situational Nature of Commitment

Within the coaching framework, commitment is somewhat "situational" and needs to be balanced with the requirements of each interaction. For example, most plans don't require an activist level of commitment. Be aware of the commitment level that is needed; then engage others and openly talk about it. If the right commitment level is lacking in your partners, share your concerns with them. Explain that you would be willing—if they would be willing—to raise the level of investment and engagement in the plan. If you and your partners are aware of the commitment level that is needed, and if it exists, then you are in good shape. If not, you need to work to achieve the synergy necessary to accomplish the plan.

The key is not to be oblivious or to ignore where people are in terms of commitment.

Some people believe that Step Four, initiating the plan, is the pay dirt, or the "end zone" of coaching. We believe, however, that experiencing a high level of commitment represents the real "pay dirt" of the coaching process. It is the culmination of the previous steps and is central to a complete coaching process. As with most of the other steps, the coach can only help "set up" a winning scenario. With commitment, the coach can test, confirm, seek out, help build, inspire, and empower. Coaches can display their commitment and their enthusiasm to the others involved.

> **However, others must come to terms with this step—with their own integrity, accountability, ownership, passion, courage, faith, and resolve.**

"Eight" Forces of Commitment

Commitment is derived from, and is built upon, a set of eight forces that influence your resolve. When these forces are strong, both you and your partner are more likely to declare your resolve. If you don't acknowledge and work in concert with these forces, the spirit, desires, and confidence essential to commitment will eventually begin to dwindle. The following sections describe these eight commitment forces:

8 Forces of Commitment
1. Ownership
2. Perceived Value
3. Autonomy
4. Validity & Reliability
5. Optimism
6. Ability
7. Resources
8. Ecology

1. Ownership

Probably the most important prerequisite or foundation of commitment is "felt ownership." Ownership is the degree to which both parties feel they have had input into the design of the plan. Many people would like to be the master architect of the agreement or plan. Generally speaking, however, genuine commitment is best achieved through balanced input and consensus. Commitment is incremental. If you worry about it only at this phase of the process, it's too late! Commitment starts with an internally felt need to seek out alternatives. It then continues to build with a plan for which both parties feel ownership and attachment.

The key here is to simply help the coaching parties understand that they are stakeholders in the plan. Ownership means that both parties acknowledge that the joint plan is true and solid. It becomes part of yourself. And, even though the plan is a shared creation, people feel that they can act independently, without assistance and without being controlled, on the portion of the plan for which they are accountable. Ownership brings with it a great set of positive feelings and becomes the key to empowerment and commitment.

While you are engaged in the coaching process, you will want to ask your partner questions like, *"Do you feel that you have had a chance to influence the shape of the plan?" "Do you feel that your ideas are reflected in our agreement?" "How much ownership do you feel for this situation?"* These, and other similar questions, will help you gauge the readiness and willingness of the other party to move forward with you.

---

2. Perceived Value

Commitments are often tied to how valuable or beneficial the plan is to the parties involved. The more the plan is connected to individual needs, aspirations, and meaningful outcomes, the more readily the commitment will be achieved. Commitment helps trigger the excitement factor and raises the level of motivation. Ofttimes, the goodness of a plan has intrinsic value: from your internal perspective, the proposed actions or solutions "feel" right and appeal to your values and principles. Solid commitments are frequently based on these belief systems. Goodness or value is also tied to extrinsic economic or material benefits. People often ask the question, "What's in it for me?" Not only is the commitment phase of the coaching process tied to the planning step, but also to the clarification of consequences, which is Step Seven. This demonstrates how the steps are interconnected.

So, in the coaching process, ask your partners to identify what benefits they see in moving forward with you on this plan. You are partially testing out a sense of commitment, but you are also bridging into a discussion of the consequences or outcomes that could be a result of effort expended. You could ask any of the following questions:

- *Do you feel this plan will meet some of your own needs?*
- *Describe how this plan will meet some of your interests.*
- *What benefits do you see accruing from this plan?*
- *What is it about this plan that makes it exciting to you?*

A high-level commitment is much more likely when there are perceived benefits, and when the proposed actions or decisions are consistent with your goals, values, and principles. This means that not only should the benefits be identified, but they need to be congruent with the vision of both parties.

---

3. Autonomy

Commitment is an emotional process—it comes from the heart—whereas the planning process is more of an intellectual process, and comes from the mind. Autonomy is *a feeling one gets when the situation is self-governing, when you can shape your share of future actions. It is a feeling of freedom and independence.*

While coaching is about partnerships, it is important to respect the need for people to feel they have some latitude and flexibility. Each party gives willingly and receives a fair measure in return, creating the sense of empowerment that is so critical to the commitment-

The commitment is a voluntary contract each party enters into. It is grounded in the legal doctrine of mutual consent and valid consideration.

Autonomy provides a sense of freedom and independence that literally puts a person in control of his or her own destiny.

building process. This facet of coaching requires that you try to clarify the other parties' feelings about their felt autonomy. This can be done simply by asking questions of this nature:

- *How do you feel about the flexibility or the latitude you have in our agreement?*
- *Are you feeling too many restrictions on this plan?*
- *Do you feel that you have enough authority and freedom to accomplish what we want to do together?*

4. Validity and Reliability

If you can crystallize in your own and your coaching partner's minds the qualities of validity and reliability, you will be much closer to sealing a high level of commitment. Validity refers to the degree to which the plan or solution is well-grounded, relevant, or meaningful—a logical conclusion that has been thoughtfully derived from the topic or situation that sparked the coaching exchange. A valid plan is appropriate; it fits, in terms of the overall situation and objectives. People think that the plan is workable when it is valid, and they believe that it will produce desirable consequences.

Reliability refers to the fact that the plan will be consistent over time, and that it will yield desirable results on a repeated basis. The plan is predictable and can be trusted. Once a person feels that this plan is not a one-shot deal but has long-term value, that it is truly logical and well thought out, you can expect higher levels of commitment. The types of questions that work nicely include the following:

- *How effective does the plan seem to you?*
- *How comfortable are you with the details of the plan?*
- *Do you think the plan will hold up over time?*

5. Optimism

Optimism is emotional support and expressed confidence—not so much in the plan, but in the person you are coaching. This facet of commitment ties into the support core. In some difficult situations, the needed optimism and emotional support—and even confidence—may have required an investment on your part. It is far easier to express confidence and emotional support for someone who operates at 110%! It is more of a risk to reach out to someone who hasn't deserved such support. In these cases, it becomes an "investment stretch." In some cases, it may be argued that it is undeserved optimism and support. The key here is to take a risk, to put it into words, and to try to *charge* and energize the commitment.

> **Undeserved Support**

> By being optimistic, you model your beliefs and commitments.

Optimism suggests your belief in what you have created; that what you have developed is the best possible initiative or response.

Try to anticipate the best possible outcome, describe it, and put it into words. When this is accomplished, you are more likely to create an upbeat vision that can be shared with others. Again, you can see how commitment begins to touch on and create a bridge for other steps, like Step Seven's clarifying of the consequences. Optimists state their level of commitment and express their faith and belief in the other person, as well as in the solution. Optimists create an environment of encouragement; help others think in positive, constructive ways; and enable them to envision success. The need for emotional support and optimistic words will vary; try to judge and balance this need in terms of whom you are working.

6. Ability

A lot of plans make sense to people and seem valid and effective. People may believe that the plan will produce results, and they have shared their ideas. However, there may be a gap in their skills or abilities, and this "ability obstacle" to commitment can be both perceived and real. Some people have had a lot of training and preparation, but have never tried doing the kinds of things that are called for in the plan. It is critical to commitment to check people's sense of their ability, knowledge, and skills to deliver on a plan.

An element of fear and anxiety may be associated with the plan. Some of this is dealt with in the next chapter on excuses and resistance. Assessing the level of commitment helps discover how much resistance exists, as well as the types of excuses and objections. It is important to ask your partners if they feel that they have the background, the experience, and the knowledge, as well as the skills, to carry out their part of the plan. When probing this, test it out gently. You might ask:

- *Do you feel comfortable, with the training you have had, doing the kinds of things that we are talking about?*

- *Do you feel that your experience will assist you in this situation?*

- *From what you know, does the plan seem doable to you?*

These questions will help draw out the level of commitment and will help indicate whether or not the coaching process needs to revert back to Step 4 and build some training experience or knowledge into the plan. If so, the parties will then be better prepared to move forward in a constructive way.

7. Resources

Every plan, agreement, or solution needs to be adequately equipped with the resources, tools, equipment, finances, and time frame to accomplish the planned mission or agreement. You simply want to test the water here, and ask the other people to describe how they feel about the time frame, etc., that has been allocated to accomplish the task at hand.

8. Ecology

No one is an island, and no plan or commitment exists in isolation. We are all connected to larger systems, and interrelationships exist between our associates, organizations, families, and society as a whole. This element of commitment encourages both parties to look at the effect the plan will have on these wider relationships or variables. You might ask:

- *Are there any adverse by-products of this commitment?*
- *Will anyone be hurt by this plan?*
- *What do we need to take action on, or give up, in order to achieve the goal?*

Step Five is a linking step between the plan on one hand and the down-range consequences on the other. We just need to remind ourselves of the basic physics principle that *every action has a reaction;* every choice

Plans and commitments are not about getting what you want at the expense of others.

has a consequence. The key here is to make sure that the actions and outcomes are in balance, or harmony, for both parties. A similar principle in physics states that *force is the result of speed, mass, and momentum.* Likewise, commitment is a function of these eight variables. Ask questions like:

- *Who else does this affect?*

- *What will happen when we achieve the result we want?*

- *Is there anything we need to change, or do we need to take the perceptions of others into account?*

By working through this step, you create a platform that will allow people to prepare to take action.

The central idea is to lock on, and be aware of, commitment levels.

Commitment is nothing more than desire or motivation in action. Commitment boils down to a vision or feeling of a plan that has not yet been actualized.

The key is to make the first move. Lao Tzu said, "The journey of a thousand miles begins with a single step."

It is what is needed to preserve existing strengths or to pursue a new or unfamiliar opportunity in the future.

If a plan is well-formed, if people believe that it is achievable, compelling, and motivating, it is likely that commitment has been achieved and the stage is set for action. Once the first step of commitment has been taken, the readiness to act, to believe, and to respond with new habits, values, and principles will be high.

We have now created the moving cause of action. Commitment rests upon the foundation of sound principles outlined above. If you do not build properly on these foundations, stated commitments will not hold up. The partners will not be true possessors of high-level commitment. Until these foundations of commitment are explored and resolved in the minds of both parties, progress will not be made.

The coaching process can easily become bogged down in analysis paralysis. Commitment is the spirit of resolve and determination, of action, and empowerment. People should feel encouraged, hopeful, upbeat, and mentally primed for action!

Most importantly, commitment is an emotional step.

Commitment is basically suggesting that you are ready to turn off the brain and turn on some adrenaline in anticipation of "going for it." Without commitment, there will simply be no creation, no proactivity.

You can't give commitment to your partners. You can't make them do it and believe it. Rather, it is preceded by good planning and preparation and is based on truth. The coaching process is designed to help explore commitment levels, to help seed the ground, to help nurture the commitment, and then to assist as it blossoms into action. Just like the farmer who plants seeds, the coach who seeks commitment must prepare the soil, till properly, fertilize, and most importantly, plant the seeds where sunshine and moisture are sufficient. All of these elements provide the framework for an abundant crop and a successful harvest. The hope is that commitment will appeal to something deep inside, and will help stir people to action, rather than having parties simply "go through the motions" like robots.

Why Don't We Ask

When coaches don't ask about commitment, it may be for fear of hearing "No," or the concern that their questions may be interpreted as "not giving their partners enough space." Fight these reservations, and if asked why you are asking, a simple response will suffice: "Because I want to know how you feel and where you stand." If commitment is nonexistent, an earlier phase of the discussion needs to be revisited: Steps One, Two, Three, and Four usually hold the keys for lack of commitment. The other alternative is that this may not be a topic for a coaching discussion; your partner may be uncoachable on this subject.

IN SUMMARY, the coach plays a vital part in bringing commitment to the relationship. A line of questions can be used to determine the commitment level of each party and to begin the process of accountability. The key here is to avoid "assumed" commitments.

Remember, commitment is always enhanced when the coach asks for, and accepts, input from others, without trying to control the process. In effect, the coach allows the others to "worry" their fair share about the plan. This can be done by asking questions such as:

- *What is the most valuable part of the plan?*
- *What is the most interesting and exciting part of the plan?*

The coach can then gently ask other parties if they are committed to carrying out the plan. A response at this point is crucial, and so the coach should listen for, and receive it. If the person exhibits non-verbal avoidance behaviors, these still constitute a response. These are the responses that lead to Step Six. The principles in Step Six will help you work through the resistance.

At this point, it would be well to specifically ask your coaching partners what the next step is, and how long it will take to get things rolling. A non-answer, or an evasive answer, is almost as informative as a direct answer.

You are not trying to manipulate or "to tip the scales" to have your partners say something they don't believe, or don't *want* to say. Above all, you want honesty.

It doesn't matter what level of commitment you get, so much as it matters that you know where you are. Then you can begin the process of strengthening the commitment.

Commitment questions are intended to gather information and to allow the other persons to express themselves. They are not intended to put down or demean others. Some of these questions may be very direct, while others are more subtle. Examples of these options might be:

- *Will you commit to this plan?*
- *Are you committed to this plan?*
- *How do you feel about this plan?*
- *Does this plan make sense to you?*
- *How does it look?*
- *Do you want to try it?*
- *Will you try it?*

As you select the style and type of questions, you need to be guided by the personality of the individuals, their track records, and the nature of the situation.

The hope is that commitment will help ignite the fire and become a catalyst for enthusiasm and excitement. Don't make the mistake of just attaching commitment to Step Four.

Keep in mind that it is important to check commitment to the relationship, role, assignment, vision, expectations, and needs surrounding the situation.

Commitment sometimes needs to be "tested out" and explored as early as Steps One and Two in the coaching process. Are the parties committed to an understanding of the current situation? Are they supportive of the future vision and overall direction? So Step Five is really an adjunct and a connecting link between many of the steps—a transition step.

This may not always be a huge step, nor does it have to take a lot of time. Perhaps the answers are "yes" or "no," but sometimes they may be lengthy explanations. It is just like the seasonings for a meal—the herbs and spices sometimes make a significant difference in the main course. So it is with Step Five. Commitment provides a very important enhancement to the overall coaching experience—not necessarily in its impact on the whole plan, but in taking the first step to get the ball rolling.

Chapter 12
Step Six: Confront Excuses and Resistance

The job of the coach is not to focus on the excuse, itself; but rather to get the other person to focus on positive actions, contingencies, or back-up plans.

The Coach

Chapter 12
Step Six: Confront Excuses and Resistance

Step Six reflects the spirit of courage. The phrase "confront excuses and resistance" may appear to be a POWER STEP, although nothing could be further from the truth. Even the term "confront" seems a bit aggressive. Confront means that we need to be honest, truthful, and courageous in bringing the detrimental and potentially disastrous effects of resistance to the forefront of the conversation.

The hope is that the excuses and resistance will be confronted with support and understanding.

The key is putting your own experiences and feelings into words and inviting inquiry into the resistance. This step is not a platform for either coaching partners to argue with the other. The bold terminology of this step is directed at resistant behavior, not at the intent or character of the people you are coaching. Confronting the excuse and not the person is, in fact, a liberating experience. Helping others overcome roadblocks, impediments, and inertia is very empowering for both parties.

Don't confuse placement with the event.

In the model, excuses and resistance are placed in the number six position. However, it is quite possible to see no excuses or resistance, to have them present at the beginning of the conversation, or to have them crop up later in your discussions.

We chose to place them where they are potentially the most harmful and, if worked through—the most beneficial, next to commitment and plans.

Why Are They Made?

Excuses and resistance are limitations that are thrust on people by their own fear and anxiety about "stepping out," or moving into a new place or in a new direction.

In Step Six, you confront the fear that you or your partner cannot precisely control future events.

If either partner is feeling some exposure or vulnerability in trying something new as part of the plan, then resistance is a normal and natural coping response.

It is natural to want to shift the burden of responsibility and attribute barriers to something or someone else. This desire will begin to manifest itself as you explore the preceding step of commitment. It may be that here you face and deal with something you do not understand and, therefore, find difficult to accept. Consequently, reservations begin to float to the surface. Step Six is the logical extension of Step Five, the commitment. If the resistance is correctly processed, this step is designed to help create more commitment for both parties.

The result of successfully working through the excuses is higher levels of COMMITMENT and tighter plans, with greater ownership!

The level of resistance is roughly commensurate with the harsh pain of reality that either party is experiencing in moving forward with change. The action or change can be viewed as a "cure" for some topic or need, and often, people develop the notion that this cure is worse than the ailment. In other words, the pain of making a change in behavior, attitude, or mindset is more difficult than the thought of living with the situation as it currently exists. The status quo

Working with ambivalence and helping others get "unstuck" is a pivotal skill for the coach.

is known, and it probably seems safe—even though in the long run, it may not be either effective or safe. People will often acknowledge that new or different initiatives are possible, but they find it hard to get cracking in a new direction. Ambivalence has set in: "I want to, but I don't want to" (or, "yes, but....").

Excuses and resistance actually perform a valuable function in the coaching process, even though on the surface they seem frustrating and obstructive. Excuses tell you if the other person feels supported. They indicate whether you have achieved "impact," Step Three in the coaching process. Excuses tell you whether the plan is truly workable, and whether the commitment is coming from the heart.

Like the other coaching steps, Step Six requires courage to engage your partner, state your observations, guide the "coping" process, and acknowledge your own resistance. Negativity, pessimism, and cynicism present a formidable challenge—a challenge that must be prepared for. Furthermore, resistance is a two-edged sword, both partners do it. Remember, both members of a partnership are capable of creating a few potholes of resistance.

Type One and Type Two Excuses

We don't have elaborate names for the two primary types of excuses and resistance, but simply call them "Type One" and "Type Two." Basically, a Type One excuse bars the two parties from discussing the topic or issue in a meaningful way and restricts the accurate gathering of data. Type Two excuses, on the other hand, prevent the parties in the coaching process from moving into genuine action.

Type One excuses are actually very simple and usually harmless. Type One excuses are more annoying than anything, while Type Two excuses can be paralyzing. One's typically manifest themselves when you focus on the topic, need, or impact and your partner wants to minimize or shift responsibility away from this sensitive discussion. Type One excuses help individuals feel better about the status quo. They represent the *novocaine of rationalization*, to help them tolerate the raw nerve of current reality. They attempt to pull standards and expectations down so that the current choices or behavior feel as if they are in alignment with desired goals or behavior. Partners may also use excuses as a means of "saving face," so the other partner will have a more favorable impression. In the medical community, two separate studies have shown that patients will complain about bodily symptoms to cover psychological or relationship problems. In fact, doctors estimate that 2/3 of their time is spent treating individuals whose real problems are not physical.

What is critical in coaching is to remember that people who use complaints as excuses are not necessarily being deceitful. Rather, they may be using the adverse circumstances that surround them to their advantage. Coaching becomes more challenging when your partners take a valid excuse or complaint too far, try to leverage it too much, try to gain sympathy or attention, or guard against the negative impressions others might form. A lot of Type One excuses are an indication that the impact hasn't kicked in. An impact void creates more denial; then defensiveness, and resistance can fill in. It feels like a yo-yo effect when you run into repetitive Type One excuses. Exposing topic or impact will often cause defensive reactions, even if the coaching opportunity does not suggest some kind of error or wrongdoing. The topic may inadvertently suggest to your coaching partner that he or she committed an error in not recognizing the opportunity. The "not invented here" mentality begins to

> People who use complaints as excuses are not necessarily being deceitful.

Although Type-One excuses are quite normal reactions, they tend to insulate people from the learning process.

breed its own unique form of resistance; that is, if I don't see the topic first or invent the solution, I won't support it.

These Type One excuses can be recognized by simply identifying the time frame of the excuse. If your coaching partner is resisting the topic by citing events and circumstances that have already occurred, you are likely experiencing the classic Type One excuse. These are caused when people feel a bit threatened, or when they perceive that others are not listening to both sides of the story. Sometimes people feel a need to go into history to prove their point, and they may use external events to justify themselves and to protect their self-esteem. The more you present the topic as a constructive, positive opportunity and look at the glass as being "half full," the less likely you are to get bogged down in Type One excuses.

For example, if you position the topic

Type-One excuses are like water under the bridge.

by saying, "Why didn't you get the assignment done in time?", you are virtually guaranteed to be inundated with Type One excuses of all varieties. If you say, "Will you help me figure out ways to decrease the turn-around time on certain projects?", you are less likely to snag a Type One excuse, simply because personal attacks or accusations are not part of this language. If you say, "Will you help me figure out how to reach a new level of customer service?" or "How can we drive out more cost, or sales?", the topic is on neutral or positive ground, independent of a "problem." If there is a problem, then make the causes of this problem a subset of the topic, and explore the cause in a very

matter-of-fact and non-aggressive manner. You might say, "Could I get your help and perspective in trying to figure out why the accident rate is increasing? I am deeply concerned about this."

The key is to focus on the topic and learn more about the root source, not to accuse or unfairly attribute it to your coaching partner.

When you point a finger at others, they generally become defensive; when you focus on the "process," it is less personal and requires less resistance.

Type Two excuses, on the other hand, are perceptions of obstacles to the carrying out of the agreement and plan; they inhibit movement. These excuses will be created or focused on to the degree that agreement and commitment seem difficult and painful. In a 1986 study by M.R. Leary and J.A. Shepperd, they described self-handicap as: "a verbal claim that a personal weakness or problem has debilitated one's performance on a task." When the self-handicap is employed on a current or future plan or agreement, individuals are trying to control the perceptions and beliefs that others have of them. If a person sets up a Type Two excuse, like illness, the day before a big assignment or test and their performance isn't as strong as was hoped for, they can rationalize and escape negative impressions. The illness "self-handicap" serves up a lower expectation and creates a mechanism for avoiding responsibility or learning.

Even perceived (imagined) constraints and novel resistance require you to work constructively through them. Again, be patient and supportive. In high-stress situations, a very good coaching technique may be to allow your partners to vent their feelings. Sometimes the excuses are a good cathartic process, and your

Partners sometimes use excuses as a "self-handicap."

Many Type-Two excuses are completely legitimate. These are real constraints, potential problems, and barriers, which need to be explored. They add value to the plan's end product.

partners will eventually come full circle. These Type Two excuses are a bit more challenging. Until you work with them for a while, it may be difficult to distinguish avoidance behaviors from genuine barriers that necessitate some rethinking and reconstruction of the plan.

Committing to, and achieving a plan, is a lot like climbing a ladder. Each step is higher and more frightening. Gravity, always resisting, is a drag on your effort to climb. Maintaining some open dialogue will give both partners the opportunity to talk about their feelings, as they climb higher and stretch further. If you listen, support, and understand, you will be able to isolate the material challenges from the merely perceived irrational excuses. You will ultimately prevent the "victim mentality" from setting in; that is, the feeling that you are out of control, that you cannot influence your destiny.

> **When you and your coaching partner can say "obstacles don't matter, we are moving ahead anyway," you have successfully processed the obstacles and resistance.**

Excuse Categories

Within the Types One and Two excuse structure, you can see categories that most excuses and resistance fall into:

Institutional

Institutional excuses focus on government, the economy, the laws, the younger generation, the top

management, the investors, and the customers. These can be very effective obstacles to accomplishment, because any one individual has little impact on large institutions. Therefore, they become convenient avenues to attempt to escape responsibility for action.

Institutional excuses represent very broad obstacles.

People

It is convenient to blame others for their shortcomings and downfalls; and it is easy to expect or anticipate that renewed efforts and plans will be effective only when others cooperate. Frequently you hear people say, "If I could only get others to cooperate, we could really move forward," or "I can't predict how someone is going to respond to this new idea." It is easy to appear helpless and at the mercy of your peers, leaders, students, customers, and so forth. The truth is, you can't control others; but you *can* influence them, positively. You can also develop processes to help offset what others do.

Human excuses present effective avoidance or escape clauses, simply because you can't control the actions, commitment, and performances of other people.

Denial

This takes many forms: arguing, hostility, interrupting, disagreeing, ignoring, silence, or excessive agreeableness. How you respond to these attempts by your partner makes the difference and is a true test of your supportiveness. Synergistic coaching will help you and your partner come to grips with the difficult obstacles.

Regardless of the form, the challenge is not to meet fire with fire.

Fears and Habits

Often, people feel that they can't move forward because they did not invent the idea, or they are unable to progress with the plan because of certain habits that restrict them from trying new ideas. They may also

Personal excuses include people's own fears, habits, idiosyncrasies, customs, and beliefs.

fear negative repercussions. Many people allow their own memory to be the scapegoat. After all, it is only human to forget. It doesn't require a decision, it just happens. For those with real memory loss or attention deficit disorders, it is a real challenge. As with all excuses, understanding needs to be combined with resourceful thinking to counterbalance the challenge.

Time

Time or clock and calendar excuses deal with the fact that people's "plates are loaded," they don't have time, they are caught in the activity trap, they are focused on reacting. They can't distinguish urgent activities from important activities. Consequently, they can get caught up in a vicious cycle of always putting out fires. They simply can't get on top of matters, and it is easy to blame the clock. They feel they just can't fit new ideas in, or they are unwilling to drop old strategies, or old paradigms, that occupy their calendar.

Knowledge

Ignorance, the lack of information, is probably one of the most convenient forms of escape.

How many times have you used the excuse that you didn't know that something was important? You protest that you didn't hear the information. You assert that you didn't realize that the speed limit was really thirty-five in this part of town. Or, you are sure that you haven't received the memo or heard the announcement. Like all excuses, it is very hard to combat, because the only person who knows for sure is the person who is offering the resistance.

Environment

The weather is probably the most popular scapegoat. In addition, road conditions, traffic, construction, accidents, supplies, material defects, etc., can be very convenient distractions. The rainfall will never be just right, the head winds will always be there. Airlines and other modes of transportation have delays, and other unexpected inconveniences intervene. You simply need to help others understand that you should plan on some "headwinds" and delays. They are all part of our complex and fast-paced society. They can't fall victim and allow the environment to paralyze them.

The environment offers plenty of escape avenues.

The Problem of Avoidance

Before getting to the process of managing legitimate Type Two obstacles and redirecting the plan, we need to say a little more about avoidance. Avoidance is the fear and hesitation associated with the unknown. You can easily become preoccupied with the fear of failure rather than the picture of success.

This preoccupation with irrational barriers represent normal avoidance that you experience every day of your life.

Avoidance is usually all emotion. You envision the worst-case scenario rather than envisioning success.

When you go to the dentist, when you anticipate the complexities of taking the test to renew your driver's license, or if you determine that it is best in the long run to change careers, you go through a range of reactions from "let's get going" to "not on your life." It is not unusual to anticipate the worst-case scenario before you actually take the driving test: You hear rumors that the test questions are all new and that if you miss more than one, you will be forced to go to an expensive and time-consuming re-certification school. Avoidance can go on and on, as there is no limit to your imagination. You can dig a hole for yourself that is impossible to get out of, and most of this "hole" is only in your mind. It isn't logical, but it is PSYCHO-

The Re-direct Approach

LOGICAL! It has a logic all right, but it can only stand up to the scrutiny of your own mind. Even when the Type Two excuse is not a manifestation of fear and avoidance, you have a great opportunity to apply the coaching process. You re-direct the excuse or legitimate reason toward some constructive, even small, action or response. Even if the help is minor, or token, it can keep things on a more positive and constructive plane.

The point is, some excuses are defensible; therefore, you don't want to make your partner defensive.

Dr. Robin Kowalski at Western Carolina University did a study in 1995 on complaints and excuses and learned that some are authentic and some are not. Authentic complaints are usually due to real feelings of dissatisfaction whereas unauthentic complaints are not. In these cases, the excuse is driven by a desire to achieve rewards of some kind (sympathy, assistance, manipulation, etc.) or to avoid punishment.

We strongly suggest that you don't spend time and effort sorting out whether or not the excuses are legitimate or superficial. The reason is because you simply handle them in the same way.

With any excuse, try to re-direct the conversation into a preventive or contingency discussion. Try to generate additional plans to prevent the obstacle in the future.

People get into trouble when they try to label excuses that seem phony or artificial. It is impossible to know for sure what is a reason and what is resistance. It causes feelings when you guess. The strategy we are suggesting treats all objections, excuses, and resistance the same.

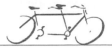

It really helps, and it teaches a sound coaching principle—that every excuse, obstacle, legitimate reason, or barrier to the plan absolutely requires some kind of response.

It doesn't really matter whether the response is perfect or not. What does matter is that you are teaching and coaching a proactive stance to life's circumstances and challenges.

Fear of Unknowns

Whenever you embark on a journey, there are inherent risks and problems about future unknowns. The fear of these unknowns, the exposure and vulnerability, is the greatest cause of resistance. Anticipation of problems and fear are normal and natural human reactions. Sometimes the plan will take you to a new place or into new "territory." Pioneering new ideas will frequently create fears and risks that come with testing out new ways of behaving. You often need to cope with the harsh reality that the action plan may inconve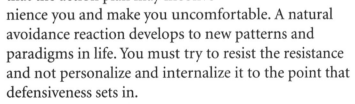nience you and make you uncomfortable. A natural avoidance reaction develops to new patterns and paradigms in life. You must try to resist the resistance and not personalize and internalize it to the point that defensiveness sets in.

To a large extent, Type Two excuses provide valuable insights into the thinking process, into potential obstacles, and into your level of commitment. These insights provide feedback on how effectively and rapidly the coaching process is working.

Type Two excuses are more substantive. They are worth learning about and exploring in detail. We say these excuses are "up-stream" because they are insights about and predictions of events that have not yet occurred and, therefore, can be addressed.

You do not need to wait to be victimized by future events and circumstances. You may not be able to completely prevent or eliminate all Type Two excuses, but you can adopt a pattern of doing something, even at a token or symbolic level, to ward off Type Two excuses and obstacles.

The key is to keep active, keep moving, and not be caught sitting and waiting for events to "catch" you. Some unforeseen events may catch up with you or may catch you off-guard. Still, you need to be determined not to go down without a fight. In coaching, you must establish the point that you have to take responsibility to minimize the probability of an excuse materializing. Keep in mind that resistance can affect both parties, and as a coach, you must be prepared to face your own special forms of resistance. So be open to help from others in working out your own excuses as well.

If, as coach, you can learn to go into the contingency-thinking mode, you can help others learn. You can help them think through the "what if's" in a constructive way. Ultimately, you can help them achieve more satisfaction and be more successful at work and in life. If you look at excuses as a valuable element of the coaching dialogue, you will begin to feel less frustrated with them. If you can identify and bring your own forms of resistance to the surface, it will be easier for your coaching partners to work their way through their own excuses and resistance.

Type One excuses will be generated partly by the way you present the topic or issue. Develop the skill to create a positive discussion environment. Look at Type Two excuses as a resource or opportunity. As we suggested during our discussion of Step Two, approach others and think of them as providing a growth opportunity or solution rather than as the obstacle or the problem itself. This approach sets the foundation for no-fault coaching. No-fault coaching focuses on the process or procedure, not the person's character.

No-Fault Coaching

Learn to appreciate Type Two excuses. They are the first signal that the plan may need adjustment, and that more patience, preparation, and thinking will be required if progress is to occur. They also mean that the two partners are really invested and engaged.

You must prepare for the possibility of the real excuses materializing and blocking the plan's progress. It is a little bit like a volleyball game. When the plan is at risk, or being spiked by excuses or resistance, you need to begin the "digging" process and keep the ball "in play." This doesn't mean that you can eradicate the excuse or that you should start a holy crusade against people who give you excuses. It just means that you need to develop a strategy to help work through preventions and contingencies.

The coaching approach teaches the principle of never giving up. It reinforces the point that you have not failed, and that the plan won't fail, until you give up trying to do something about the excuse.

It teaches you to refuse to allow yourself to become a victim or co-conspirator without a struggle. It is really a foundation principle in our society. It is the reason that 50 million people are encouraged to vote, despite the fact that one individual vote seems, on the surface, to be so insignificant. It is the principle that makes a difference over time.

Response Options

What are the keys? How do you handle excuses in a coaching fashion? People handle excuses in five basic ways. Although they may not all be appropriate, we are simply describing a broad range of methods you can choose from.

Option One

One of the methods of handling an excuse is to simply listen to it, and then ignore it. This is not all that dramatic, but just listening and venting may help.

It is amazing, but sometimes, if you handle the resistance supportively and create a little space, commitment will grow naturally and resistance will die a natural death. Press too soon or too hard and the resistance struggles to live.

Option Two

Another response is to attack and put the excuse down with power and authority, as in the statement, "I think that is a ridiculous point." Not surprisingly, this approach is rarely effective and not very consistent with synergistic coaching. It creates the "vertical relationship," as well as resentment and unresolved feelings.

Option Three

The third approach is generally as ineffective. It involves arguing and debating with the other person on the logic and the benefits of implementing the plan, or accepting the topics. An example of arguing

would be, "But let me point out for the third time that in an article I read, it said we should do it." This debate approach is overused and can become manipulative.

As we have touched on earlier, the fourth and more coaching-oriented response is to "redirect." This involves redirecting the energy and communication into a more positive, forward-thinking posture. A friend of ours has often said: "If you are getting lemons, go into the lemonade business." Look for the silver lining that is inherent in nearly every situation. Try to see whether constructive and substantive actions can be taken to prevent further potential problems from disrupting the plan. Or you may want to find contingency or back-up plans that will minimize the overall impact of possible adverse events that would hinder progress of the agreements being made. For example, "You have a good point. This won't work unless we do some training to go with it. What are your ideas on how the training can be accomplished?"

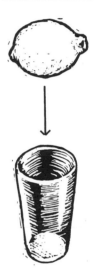

> These responses may result in a plan that is new, different, or smaller than expected—but it will be a plan, nonetheless. Redirecting gets across the notion that both parties—not just one—must accept the challenge of managing the blockers and stoppers of action.

Those who have learned martial arts understand the concept of using the energy of the other person to help in self-defense. And even though coaching doesn't always involve a conflict, another person's energy can be used to effectively combat avoidance or resistance. It can be gently and subtly redirected into productive uses.

Option Five

The fifth and final approach is to surface and "name" the excuse in objective and descriptive terms, put "light" around it, support the other persons, and see if they are willing to try something. It is the act of stating the obvious resistant behavior. In effect, you "call it out." You make it the topic of discussion. Be prepared to offer support, then be ready to start the redirect process, and most of all, expect some denial if your observations are accurate.

People are sometimes surprised and quick to discount the accuracy and power of the "naming" method. They may feel temporarily awkward or embarrassed. Be generous with support if they seem exposed when you do name it.

These approaches work if the resistance is not a calculated or preplanned move. It also helps if the excuse is not a deeply ingrained habitual pattern. Generally, exposure to the light of open discussion will help reduce the grip of resistance in a healthy way. Exposing or calling out the resistance may cause it to dissipate naturally. This occurs when the person who is resisting sees the hesitation for what it is and feels the support from the other person. Coaching partners will see the resistance if someone points it out in a synergistic way.

The central coaching message is that the absence of action and the presence of resistance are not healthy situations for the partnership. There is no escape from difficulties and harsh realities.

John Paul Jones captured the spirit of this step while his ship was burning in a naval battle with the British during the Revolutionary War. When asked if he would surrender, you may remember his famous response: "I have not yet begun to fight!"

If you can help instill a little bit of John Paul Jones' spirit and encourage others to keep trying, then you are living the coaching process. Even in sports, it is shameful for any coach to allow his team to give up, or to let down—even when they are in a "blow out." In fact, that is the insight which synergistic coaching is trying to instill: that life is all about putting up a great struggle, regardless of whether or not you are on top. This point is, if you have the energy and capability to think of an excuse, you probably have the energy and capability to begin working on some remedies.

If partners are committed, excuses and obstacles really don't matter.

The goal of confronting excuses and resistance is not to create a battle by refuting or denying the excuse. Steps like number Six and Seven require us to think ahead and add some new ideas to the plan or agreement. This step is not about attacking or putting down the other person. These approaches will only feed the resistance fire. You are not saying the other person is wrong or is behaving badly. You are simply trying to communicate and share your observations in a relaxed and accepting way. Your partners may see it differently, and there may be other angles and points to consider before the commitment is solidified.

Productive Focus

Whether the excuses are strategic, organized, planned, or deliberate; or if unorganized, random, unconscious, and/or unintended, the coaching process provides a productive way to keep the conversation focused. It acknowledges that some excuses are resolvable and

You must begin with the assumption that the excuse is not a lie.

logical. You need to recognize that people have lives, that things happen to them.

This step is not about legitimacy; it is about determination, creativity, and advance planning. It focuses on persistence and the need to help the relationship maintain a positive vision of moving forward, even if this movement is done in small, symbolic steps. You may not finish all the plans, agreements, and changes that you want; but you can't finish any journey unless you begin. Even meaningful journeys will have moments that frighten you. This step is concerned with how your thought process can hinder the action phase of coaching.

If it appears that legitimate excuses block your plan's validity, then you need to "go with the flow" and adapt. Be responsive to true potential problems. They really don't change anything in your approach. Treat both legitimate and illegitimate excuses in the same coaching way. That is, exercise your listening skills, provide logical interaction, and explore all points and arguments. Redirect the energy if it becomes negative. Finally, surface and name the resistance, and allow the light to point the way.

Problems begin to occur when you overuse some approaches and argue too long or too hard. Tension develops if you try to manipulate by "selling" too much, or if you ignore the other person's point. You get into an unrelenting "rut," and the other person will begin to resist you and your methods more than the issue or excuse that you are trying to address.

This is not a quick fix.

You can't expect immediate results with any of these approaches. It takes time for the method to work, for the message to "sink in," and for trust to build up.

> **Resistance and excuses are a natural part of the growth process. The coaching process will help you work through it, rather than cursing, rescuing, or embarrassing people who exhibit resistant behavior.**

Clarification

Some people incorrectly assume that conflict and resistance are one and the same. However, because they are different, they must be handled differently. Excuses and resistance are emotional and often unconscious choices to react in an overly cautious way to a proposal. Conflict deals with the substance of the plan, its term and content.

One friend shared this insight: *"When someone suggests to me that it is time for a dental exam, I subconsciously react and suddenly invent other things I must do. I am not arguing the merits of regular dental hygiene, but I really should consult my schedule. I react a little out of the fear of being exposed to the pain, as well as to the expense of such a visit. I often exaggerate these things to the point of postponing my visit. I need a coach. If I don't get coaching, if I get coercion, demands and threats from my partner, then I can even sink into the defiant mode. I am beyond conflict, beyond resistance. I am resolute. I am not going simply because I feel someone is requiring or forcing me to go."*

> **Adults like their autonomy and freedom. When a partner denies this, the determination to defy is strengthened. A coaching situation has been successfully turned into a stalemate.**

Don't lose sight of the support step. Support must work in tandem with the processes described above.

Check in with your support level, and make sure you are not shutting off rapport with the other individual. When dealing with behavior that is getting hard to handle, remember that occasional silence is golden. Often, the blockage or resistance will emerge with a little patience, and by allowing the other person to feel the power of silence after you have named the resistance or have redirected an excuse, you can help keep things moving.

Remember that when people feel that events are outside of their control, life can appear hopeless. No one enjoys being held hostage or feeling victimized. Redirecting the energy into some small areas that are controllable may convert the excuse or resistance into a desire to keep trying.

What If Resistance Continues?

Magic won't
cut through
the resistance.

Resistance is either a reaction or a choice made, either consciously or subconsciously, by the other person. Even in the face of all your good-faith efforts, there is **no magic dust** that will cut through resistance. Make two to three good-faith efforts to confront or shine the light, and then recognize that the person may becoming entrenched. Two approaches are possible. First, move to Step Seven and objectively clarify the consequences. Making the outcomes vivid may "jump start" the conversation onto a productive course.

The second approach is to conclude that this is not a coachable moment and that other approaches may be more productive. Examples could include seeking third party help or encouraging the other person to seek out a coach other than yourself with whom they feel more comfortable. Don't just quit; seek out more productive alternatives. This may be the only help you can provide.

Chapter 13
Step Seven:
Clarify Consequences;
Don't Punish

Clarifying consequences represents a dual-edged sword. One edge—the appropriate side—will result in the person clearly understanding the outcomes, and desiring to give the agreed-upon plan a valiant try.

The Coach

Chapter 13
Step Seven: Clarify Consequences; Don't Punish

+

OR

-

Step Seven in the coaching process symbolizes the spirit of the future. This step is one of the most misunderstood. Its heart is clarity and candor, not punishment and threats; yet, sometimes this step is perceived as a harsh and insensitive part of the coaching process. Rather, it is designed to be a "reality check" for the future, even though no one can totally predict the future or guarantee an outcome. Consequences generate interest and bring attention to the plan; they create a vision of the fruits of future success. Consequences can be expressed in either positive or negative terms or not at all. The approach depends on the level and type of commitment individuals have to the action plan.

Many people look at this step and see a power play, or the heavy use of authority. The intent of this step is not for the coaching participants to "take the gloves off" or to "play hard ball." It is neither a punching contest, nor a time to chastise or reprimand. Actually, it can be as natural and gentle a step as any. Certainly, it can be the "heavy," if the parties decide to look at it from that perspective. Generally, this step can be seen as positive and upbeat. People need to think about the positive outcomes and gains that can be achieved down the road, as opposed to the negative outcomes. As time passes, motivation will be needed to continue pursuing the plan.

This is the point in the coaching process at which you need to explore where the plan will go, and what the commitment can produce. The question is whether the plan will produce value and satisfy the needs of the two parties, as well as the needs of the team as a whole. All too often, the resolutions and actions focus on solving individual's needs rather than those of the group.

This step will show the parties in the coaching process payoffs and the positive value of their commitment.

Step Seven is different than Step Three. Many people have asked about the difference between Step Three and Step Seven. One of the main differences is that Step Three deals with the internal "decision" to act, to change, or to improve. The energy for Step Three results from parties seeing gaps between current reality and desired reality, current efforts and needed efforts, progress and goals, and intentions and results. This awareness raises the level of sensitivity around the topic and the willingness to discuss plans.

Step Seven, on the other hand, increases sensitivity and heightens motivation to act, engage, and pursue a plan. An important leap has been made from the more abstract world of designing solutions to the more concrete world of action and implementation. Step Seven is the reinforcement to form solid habits. This step looks into the future, to where the plan is leading and how it ties the individuals' personal purpose and mission to the team's purpose and mission.

> **Step 7**
> **The Insurance Policy for the Plan**

Step Three focuses the mind on new angles so that coaching partners can see the current situation, and where it is leading. It is a lot like driving a car. Mid-course changes may be needed. Mileposts suggest the driver may be off target, ahead of schedule, or behind schedule. Small or large adjustments are made. Sometimes, the driver adjusts direction by nudging the steering wheel. Other times, the car is turned around, a new route is taken, and the destination is altered.

> **The coach helps navigate and support, but does not
> become an obnoxious back-seat driver. Nor does
> the coach grasp the wheel and take control.**

In Step Four, then, the best plan of action is determined. Step Seven looks down the road at the tangible
and intangible results of the plan. In other words, this
step provides the answer to that all-important question: "What, substantively and precisely, do we think
our actions will get us?" The operative word in Step
Seven is "clarify." It doesn't say "administer" consequences.

External Consequences

Often the consequences of following through on an
action are "external" in that you usually do not have a
lot of personal control over consequences, especially
the natural variety. In Step Three, you individually
have a lot more choice about whether you want to
recognize and acknowledge the impact, consider other
viewpoints and perspectives, and then have the impact
catch your attention.

> **The important thing about Step Seven is that it
> looks to the future. As has been stated previously,
> it is a lot easier to shape the future than to try
> to reshape the past.**

Two Types of Consequences

Consequences come in two forms. First, there is the
natural variety. These are the likely natural result of a
course of action. Regardless of whether they are
positive or negative, these consequences are largely
governed by nature. Certain physical and social givens
underlie actions and reactions within the real world. If

certain actions are followed, they should result in safe and productive activity. If these governing ideas are not followed, resistance, conflict, and pain are likely outcomes.

The second type of consequence is imposed by other humans or their institutions. These consequences are more mechanical. The cause and effect are controlled by people and the way they can reward and discipline. For example, in a business, if a plan does not meet the needs of the parties, the players may disengage or leave the team. If the plan does meet the future needs of the coaching partners, you can expect to see greater levels of interest and enthusiasm. If the plan does not meet needs or produce results that are considered central and critical to the integrity and survival of the team, then the parties need to understand the nature and scope of the harmful or distasteful consequences.

As with other steps in the coaching process, this step needs to have a left-to-right flow on the consequence continuum. Starting to the left of center, the long-range positive consequences can be explored from the perspective of all parties. Discover the consequences together. Try to assess how these consequences are affecting commitment and motivation. Ask:

- *How do you see this plan paying off?*
- *What risks exist?*
- *How will a lack of plan success block us from reaching our needs or achieving our vision?*

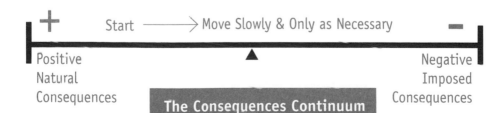

The Consequences Continuum

It is easy to start on the left side in that any negative consequences can be approached from the positive side. For example, you can say, "If we make the sale, here is how everyone wins," rather than saying, "You know, if we don't get this sale, you will have to take a draw." If the left side is not producing energy, **gradually** test out the right side.

The key is to have no surprise.

Sometimes, your emotions and frustrations drive you to the right side, or to the negative consequences. For example, if your message to a team member is, "If you don't follow these uniform safety practices, you will face disciplinary action," you could instead say, "You know, when you and all of us support the safety code of conduct, it makes this place a lot more enjoyable to work in, and we reduce the risk of hurting our most valuable asset—our people!" Your colleagues hear the positive first. They should understand the good consequences, as well as the harm that could come from not being in alignment with the plan. What would it be like to have a truly safe environment where people really cared?

Be clear; don't let others guess. It is essential to transform the mindset from the present to the future. The key word is *forecast* or *project,* not *dictate* or *impose.*

Step Seven requires good judgment, thought, and skill as you introduce both positive and negative consequences into the dialogue. This step is designed to explain what is at stake. Don't engage in saturation bombing with threats. With the coaching process, you want to drive out fear, and yet, you don't want to hide from the reality of consequences. Every choice has a consequence. If this step is addressed in a non-punitive fashion with a spirit of empathy and support, the coaching process will produce motivation and power.

Consistency and fairness is essential. This step is fragile and delicate in the sense that you do not want to raise defense barriers. You can avoid a lot of prob-

lems if you constantly state your intention to provide clarity and objective information for your partner. Clarify that you are not interested in being insensitive or harsh. The intent is not to single out someone for attack, but rather to discover and share the benefits and risks of a plan, or a lack thereof.

You are not trying to imply that the plan will be easy but that it is worthwhile.

Step Seven is similar to Step Three, in the sense that the types of motivators and exciters that build your interest to interact and think about a plan will also spark your drive to execute the plan. In reference to Maslow, your future plans and actions can have a positive or negative effect on your needs for survival, security, social and self-esteem, and personal fulfillment. With this framework in mind, you can look at long-term consequences from these perspectives.

Depending on individual differences and cultural diversity, the consequences may or may not spark an important need.

This step helps people see the following:

- *What is in it for me?*
- *What is the plan worth?*
- *What is in it for my coaching partner?*
- *How does the team win?*

Be genuine in this step; don't fabricate or exaggerate. Instead, try to figure out what it will take to sustain the new effort, plan, or agreement over time.

Knowing the people you associate with is central to this step. The better you know them, the more likely you are to have insight about their "hot" buttons. This will help you contribute to a meaningful discussion about the important and urgent consequences. Help each other make the linkages between today's actions and the future payoffs.

Explore what is at stake and what has value to the coaching partners. Examine the probabilities. Don't

make guarantees. If you want a guarantee, you should buy a toaster. Help insure that consequences are timely. You can create enormous drive and energy with this approach.

> **In synergistic coaching, it doesn't matter who receives the credit. If the plan is even partially successful, everyone becomes a beneficiary.**

Given the amount of knowledge and information that exists on the subject of motivation, it is amazing how infrequently we see this step being applied prior to sharing the coaching model with groups attending our seminars and workshops. On average, over the past ten years, less than ten percent of the coaching samples we gathered on audio tapes contain some reference to positive or negative consequences. Again, while the power of future consequences may be common knowledge and clear in the minds of many, its discussion is not common practice, nor is it clear in the dialogue and interactions we have observed. If the consequence step isn't effective in helping with change, something is amiss in the relationship. Remember the reference to the nature of a good "contract"—each party enters with the understanding of mutual consent and valid consideration. Take a look; if your associates are not getting something back, if there isn't an interest, if there is no benefit, the plan, agreement, or relationship may be in serious trouble.

Chapter 14
Step Eight: Don't Give Up!

The notion of not giving up occurs in two different time frames. The first is while talking with a partner; the second is the follow-through after the meeting.

The Coach

Chapter 14
Step Eight: Don't Give Up!

First and foremost, Step Eight is about persistence. It embodies the coach's commitment to hang in there, to devote the needed energy and time to the synergistic coaching process. So in a sense, don't give up has two meanings. One meaning focuses on the coaching style and values. The second focuses on the individual you are assisting. Others may test your sincerity. How you act and interact will confirm your commitment to a synergistic coaching and a learning relationship. This step, more than any of the others, has been difficult to put a name on. At times, we have thought of describing this step as "follow through" or "continuing." It incorporates a variety of coaching dimensions that should not be dismissed, even though this is the last element in the coaching model. In fact, to some degree, the nature of this step represents one of its paradoxes, because some people see this step as the beginning or "launching-off point" of synergistic coaching—not the ending point. If you subscribe to the notion that coaching is a process, not an event, you will see why this step is really the beginning of the process.

The Spirit of Not Giving Up

The spirit of Step Eight is one of follow-through and validating commitments. This step represents the need to plan for celebration of small steps and progress toward the ultimate objective. All too often in life, celebrations are held off until arrival at some magical

 point or destination. Step Eight is suggesting that you need to celebrate departure and the journey, as well as the destination. All too often, people fail to recognize when they have arrived, and so the celebrations are either anticlimactic, or even non-existent.

One organization we work with was unwilling to acknowledge steps toward success and celebrate, simply because they feared that members of the organization would relax their efforts and assume that they had "arrived" and throttle back on effort. Whenever possible, you must enjoy the journey as much as the destination. The other key dimension to this step is to help both parties mentally prepare for success. In other words, you need to begin to mentally rehearse the steps even in a mechanical way. In addition, you need to begin talking about what progress and success looks and feels like.

The key here is to celebrate winning—the process of success—as well as the win itself.

High-performance individuals see progress and success in their minds before they start to work. They picture it and they generate mental images. This is a vital part of the coaching process. A successful high jumper from years ago, Dwight Stones, would close his eyes and experience the jump long before he would take the first step toward the crossbar. The basketball player, Michael Jordan, does the same thing before he shoots each free throw. At times, this may be a visualization, and other times it may be his own internal coaching dialogue.

In coaching, you help yourself and the other party begin the positive dialogue and visual images before the conversation is over. Some people must have hard and undeniable evidence before they get into a positive pattern. With this final step, instead of believing that they are headed for success only when they see it, you must try to help others believe it before they see it.

Believe it before you see it.

The Accountability Factor

Accountability is an important ingredient in synergistic coaching. This is where follow-up plays a central role. The intent is not to smother the relationship with supervision and monitoring, but it is critical to keep ongoing contact alive and then be prepared to re-plan, support, and recommit on a regular basis.

If you are truly dealing with important issues, you should try to set the follow-up place, date, and time. This should be somewhere between two hours and two days from the end of the coaching discussion.

In a supportive and positive way, you want to help ensure that the commitments are honorable and that the agreements have integrity.

This step is the reassurance that effort is as important as success, and that a lack of success means it is time to regenerate and develop new ideas, action plans, and strategies. This is how you give or restore your commitment to the process and to the other person.

When we say "Don't give up," you are being encouraged first and foremost not to give up on the coaching process, or on the first approach. Don't let your emotions or others distract you or push another approach. You must learn to trust and honor this process. Secondly, you do not want to give up on the other persons. Verbally allow the other parties to know that you will "stay with it" as long as they are willing to do so. This is a key and a very special commitment that is just a little different from the commitment in Step Five, which is a commitment to the action plan, decision, strategy, or resolution.

You want to "hang in there" a lot longer than they anticipate.

Let the other persons know that the coaching
dialogue and contact will stop ONLY if they choose
to pull the plug by giving up and walking away.

Are There Times When You Do Give Up?

Above all, you must keep in mind that behavior change is evolutionary, not revolutionary. Deep and important change rarely happens overnight, which makes follow-up critical. You cannot force the coaching process onto others. But you can remain loyal and dedicated to the coaching principles and skills. In being practical, you know that there are some cases in which the coaching process is not the right "fit."

If you have a situation that is not appropriate for coaching, then don't defeat yourself and the process by trying to make coaching work. After three good-faith efforts, you can acknowledge that the situation may be trying to tell you something. Every once in a while, you will see extreme cases. Some people are not into growth, learning, collaboration, and teamwork. People who are self-destructive may need a lot of professional help to stop the entropy. Even then, however, studies support the idea that professional helpers can have only a very limited effect on those who are determined not to support the relationship—or themselves for that matter. We hope you grasp the spirit of the message. Don't give up too soon. Try to go as long as it serves the needs of the mission or task that the relationship is serving. Go as long as learning is occurring. In a learning relationship, the members are willing to live with some false starts.

Be Coachable

Before each coaching dialogue is complete, it is advisable to leave on a note of inquiry. Seek out some feedback on your performance in using the coaching process. This feedback doesn't necessarily have to be elaborate or extensive. You simply need to ask a few basic questions, such as:

- *How did this discussion work for you?*
- *Are you getting what you need?*
- *How can I help support your efforts?*
- *Was I too direct?*
- *Do you feel I have been clear, or has the agenda been too confusing?*

These types of questions and discussions will do a lot to ensure that your intentions are clear and that you have demonstrated your active interest in being "coachable." Then, take the person's suggestions to heart. Let him or her know that your commitment is to improve on your part and to make a significant contribution to a productive learning relationship. When people know that you are committed and that they are supported, you can expect to see plans and commitments achieved. In some cases, people will test first before they are willing to make the plan work out. Your durability and patience will be under the microscope.

Maintaining a healthy coaching relationship is more important than any one single topic or agreement.

You can't do too much of this step. You can't help, teach, communicate, and follow-up too much on synergistic coaching. Try to generate some positive contact on a regular basis. This should be done as soon as possible after the initial agreements or issues are discussed. This then puts your verbal signature to the

coaching process. After seeking out some feedback on the quality and effectiveness of the coaching process, ask the other person if they are getting what they want from the relationship. See if the dialogue is working for them, and if they would like anything different in the next meeting. Stress to your partner that this is the beginning of the process, not the end.

Talk that does not end in any kind of action is better suppressed altogether.—
Thomas Carlyle Inaugural Address-Edinburgh University, Scotland 1866

Observe the next discussion carefully. If there is not as much success as you would have expected, don't panic.

Re-huddle, retrace the steps in the coaching process, and try to discover where the breakdown is occurring. Emphasize again to your partner that you haven't failed until you give up trying. This is the time to rekindle the persistence and resolve to get things moving.

The first sign of visible action is critical because it begins to show the commitment. Try to build excitement and enthusiasm. Connect to Step One, and let your partners know that they are supported and okay. Make sure that you check in to ensure that the real issue, not simply the symptoms or the immediate critical incident, is clear.

As you wrap up the conversation, thank the other person for participating with you. Ask when the next conversation will be. It certainly doesn't need to be a full-blown meeting. Try to maintain the excitement. Facilitate and debrief the meeting. Ask yourself if you are getting everything you need, and if you are feeling "enrolled."

Trust

This step is ultimately designed to build trust—trust is a function of the things you believe and whether or not you are willing to express what you think and to act in accordance. In addition, trust hinges on the degree to which you accept the other person as a human with differences and imperfections. Also, you must be willing to be open, honest, and committed to mastering the positive things you are trying to bring to or do in the relationship.

It is hard to reduce synergistic coaching and partnership building to Eight Steps. But it does help, and it provides a template that the mind can easily remember after some effort and practice.

Try to agree on a location. At a symbolic level, it may be useful to meet on a "mutual" court or let your partner pick the place. Sometimes there is a perceived "home court" advantage if only one partner consistently selects the location.

Just a note as we conclude this chapter about the coaching model. It takes two people to "tango" and it takes two people to create synergy. If you get in the habit of using the coaching model regularly, people will warm up to it. In fact, the results from a year-long survey of people at all levels in ten different companies show a dramatic pattern. Out of 63 coaching questions, people consistently rate their belief in, and preference for, coaching higher than any set of questions we ask. Clearly, people want to be treated as a "coaching" partner. They believe it enhances their performance, commitment, and satisfaction. Despite these impressive results, you may encounter some

initial resistance. Some people who have been nur-
tured and reinforced on a command-and-control
model may be hesitant to work with you. They may
have adjusted to a power and authority relationship by
becoming dependent and marginally interested. They
may see the coaching approach to decision making,
action planning, and problem solving with some
doubts or suspicion. They may misperceive coaching
as a fad or an attempt to patronize when they have
experienced more abrupt and rougher tactics. You
need to trust the process. Over time, these feelings will
gradually evaporate as people feel the high involvement and genuine values that lie deep inside the
model.

Chapter 15
Creating a "Learning Relationship"— Eight Wrap-Up Points

Good coaching depends on everyone sharing in leadership. Good leadership is a unique phenomenon in any organization.

The Coach

Chapter 15
Creating a "Learning Relationship"— Eight Wrap-Up Points

Point Number 1

Welcome to our last chapter. We know that for many, your time may be exhausted, and so we doubly appreciate your decision to dig further into this subject. To make this a wise investment of time, we hope you will now move beyond reading, and that you give these ideas a test drive. All too often, developing our knowledge and people skills is not the most urgent priority in our lives. However, in Dr. Jan Halper's study, it is reported that 2/3 of 4,000 successful people in business want more interaction with their work partners and depend on interaction and coaching for their success. We hope that you have found a few specific ideas that will help you make interactions a true learning experience.

Developing good relationships is a life-long journey. The more we study consensus building and collaboration, the more we are reminded how challenging it is to make them a part of our relationships. We wish you the best as you search for ways to continually improve in this fascinating field. The effort you make to become a good partner will take you a long way toward achieving your goals.

Point Number 2

Until recently, the word "coach" has had basically one meaning: a person, usually a man, whose job was to guide the development of an athlete's skills—then to direct and enhance this athlete's contribution to the team. This enhancement was accomplished through athletic competition. Even today, Webster defines a coach as someone who trains athletes or athletic teams. To its credit, the dictionary does go on to include persons who give private instructions or who assist others in various endeavors.

As you go forward, be aware that some coaches in the very popular, athletic arena are yellers and screamers. They are focused on one thing: winning at all costs. Far too many are into short-term relationships where partnership and synergy is not the goal.

Larry Brown, a person who has coached at all levels (including pro basketball) and who was a player on the '64 U.S. Olympic Team, sees himself as a teacher rather than a sports coach. Sure, he is driven, but he is driven to achieve quality by "playing the game right" and bringing out other's talents. Brown says,  "I just want to help players get better; when you do that, good things happen." One of his team members said, "Brown doesn't take winning all that seriously. He says if we play the game right, winning will take care of itself." Coaches like this are an oddity. Brown's theory is that learning is a never-ending process, even for veteran players. Ironically, Brown says his real passion is for coaching young players. Brown has quietly developed a reputation for making bad teams good and good teams great. But, despite his bottom-line success, he is hardly mentioned as one of basketball's top coaches. He doesn't seek the limelight; he is not a flashy individual.

Keep in mind that coaching seeks to make our work-place, and our world, better places in which to live. This is accomplished by controlling others less and by being more creative as we search for synergy and win-win agreements with others.

The following definition of coaching may be useful in the future. It is the one that attendees in our seminars appreciate the most. It may be useful to keep this in mind as you think about the ideas in this book.

In the final analysis, coaching is an interaction process between members of a team (leaders to members, peers to peers, members to leaders). The goal is to positively influence behavior as well as to create relationships that are meaningful. Coaching helps raise awareness of new opportunities to develop and grow. Coaching partners strive for mutual learning, continuous improvement, and superior results.

The ultimate power of coaching rests *not* in demand-ing or in commanding others. The heart and soul of coaching lie in the helping, listening, trusting, and collaborating that are possible when two people become "learning partners." True partners depend on each other in order to function in ways that optimize their performance. In a good learning relationship these partners try to figure out how best to respond to each other and to overcome obstacles. Synergistic coaching combines support and openness to achieve breakthroughs and overcome adversity, as well as to gain a sense of personal satisfaction.

The art and practice of coaching draws on a framework of special skills, knowledge, and abilities.

As authors, we are dedicated to the future discovery and refinement of this coaching framework.

It is our heartfelt belief that in our increasingly complex walks of life, we, as *coaches*, need the courage, the confidence, and the skills to successfully meet others eye-to-eye and heart-to-heart, in order to create the conditions for helpful, respectful, and honest dialogue. As the requirements for success change and grow, so must our ability to communicate, to motivate, and to learn from each other.

Each of our partners has unique insights.

They have "special knowledge" that they can share. At times, our partners may not even be aware of this information and knowledge until we engage them. The ability to combine experiences and insights enables us to compete and to confront more challenging situations.

Remember that while our dynamic, changing world is calling for effective partnerships, our instincts may be telling us to "pull in" and to keep our opinions, insights, and perceptions to ourselves. It is easy to follow the safe path by not giving feedback to others, by not helping them discover their performance or learning "blind spots," by not drawing attention to growth opportunities, and by not helping them overcome resistance to personal reflections and change. In fact, in the findings from the Jan Halper study (cited earlier), 5 out of every 7 managers said they would rather lie than initiate honest coaching on key issues. Out of the five, almost 50% said they lacked the skills, 35% were afraid of not being liked or of conflict, and 15% hoped for automatic improvement in others. Only 2 out of 7 said they would coach honestly. In this group of two, more than 2/3 said it was because their job **required** it, and less than 1/3 felt that developing others was an **important** aspect of their role.

When you are coaching, you know enough to know that you don't know everything.

As learning partners, we also need to guard against the temptation to be heroes, to demonstrate our power or our authority, and to "go it alone." Win-win partners know how to guide, share, influence, ask questions, effectively listen, combine ideas, and facilitate the coaching process. A person in a coaching role simply guides and helps carry the process along, but doesn't control it.

Either knowingly or subconsciously, we each collaborate in setting the direction and tone of our relationships. The quality and tone of our relationships is deeply connected to the success of our lives and society. Improvements and exciting breakthroughs will occur when people care enough to effectively engage each other in helpful discussions. The groups and teams we belong to must produce quality, and they must continually improve.

To succeed in the future, organizations must coordinate many functions and "take care of the customers"—both the internal and external ones. In addition, they must balance internal control and continuity with creativity and freedom. Organizations must function safely and in harmony with their community and environment. Organizations must find a way to develop, motivate, and empower their members. The "musts" for organizations are not going to be accomplished if the communication framework is infected with the viruses of resentment, indifference, insensitivity, or benign neglect. One way to meet the challenges of the future is to nurture learning partnerships.

Point Number 3

While the need to build meaningful partnerships is clear, many of us rarely look in the mirror. Henry P. Sims and Dennis A. Gioia describe a phenomena called a self-serving bias. That is, individuals tend to accept personal responsibility for success, but attribute shortcomings, letdowns, or upsets to external causes. Similarly, M.D. Alicke and Associates in a 1992 study found that people are more likely to complain about events or people outside of themselves than take some personal responsibility. For self-preservation purposes, people hesitate to implicate themselves because they fear that others may form negative impressions[1]. This **self-serving** bias enables our own self esteem to grow artificially and allows us to avoid disapproval. It helps us fill our need for security and self-preservation. On the downside, however, is the fact that it eclipses growth opportunities. It helps us escape the constructive tension that fuels bright ideas and creative juices. When conflict ensues, we see our view as the one that

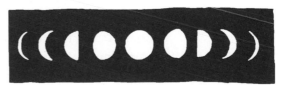

The self-serving bias eclipses growth opportunities.

is politically correct; the other is dearly misunderstood and needs to be convinced. We fall into the pit of arguments and proof. We have a difficult time climbing out and retaining a listening ear. It takes a lot of maturity and trust in the relationship to be vulnerable and open to insight and introspection, and to reflect honestly on our style, effort, and intentions.

If groups can create a safe environment, relationships can focus on understanding each other's perceptions and viewpoints. We can then put ourselves in a learning position.

Point Number 4

We can make our groups and organizations wonderful entities capable of doing tremendous good. On the other hand, they can become painful and blistering places which make it difficult for individuals to contribute to the team or to achieve their lifelong desires and aspirations.

Organizations and members need the knowledge, skills, and abilities to take the abrasive edge off their communications, problems, and problem-solving efforts.

Many pivotal factors can assist a person in bringing the learning relationship and learning organization to pass. First is the communication framework, or communication culture. Central to this framework is the personal sense of responsibility that people must feel in order to establish an effective style of communication. In truth, the communication framework is not something that corporate headquarters sends out nor can it be purchased from an expert. Instead, the framework is a function of the members of the organization, the norms they choose to create, the skills they develop, and the environment they establish. As coaches, we have the responsibility to influence the direction—as well as the destiny—of our organizations. In order to do this, we must help create and sustain a positive communication framework. The ideas you have read about should help you flesh out and develop this framework.

Point Number 5

Synergy and learning have a price. It takes a concerted effort. A person cannot effectively engage in a partnership process without dedication and vigor. It is not a casual or subconscious activity, but requires rigorous and devout commitment to the principles and values of constructive dialogue. As authors, we are painfully aware that it is easy to "walk the talk" in *theory* —to be brave, effective, and proactive *in our minds*. It is easier and very tempting to postpone the work, and to ignore coaching opportunities. To continue on in our relationships as we have always done can feel falsely comfortable to us.

In contrast, helping and supporting people to clarify and pursue their own visions, healing old wounds, continuously improving, and empowering and taking risks are not easy tasks. Helping others to sort things out and take responsibility by sharing useful feedback and information takes deep personal commitment and skill. It takes persistence because sometimes our partners will resist assuming responsibility, facing accountability, and collaborating with us. A person must decide in his or her mind and heart to become a successful coaching partner. One must be willing to learn, to be both open-minded, and action-oriented. Successful coaching requires a willingness to accept support and to be coached.

One must decide that being a little more vulnerable, a little less arrogant, a little less egotistical, and a little more flexible is the right way to approach life.

Now that you have read this book, we hope that you will agree that, over the long haul, coaching is worthwhile. There is simply no way to shift the burden of coaching and dialogue onto someone else, not through policies or well-intended procedures or programs. Coaching is a personal thing.

It doesn't have to be done perfectly, but it must be applied by individuals who have sincere and genuine intentions.

Point Number 6

Reasons not to coach can always be found.

As we see it, the main problem that prevents people from learning to coach effectively is the natural predisposition not to do so. The process of *coaching* and *caring* often goes against much of what we were taught in our youth: to be rugged and independent—to be competitive and to win individually—even at the expense of others! In Halper's study, 70% of the managers surveyed spent a great deal of time focusing on their own self-fulfillment and inward thoughts. She theorized that many people are lonely and are afraid of being upstaged by their partners and associates. They often pick weak partners to protect themselves, partners who don't stimulate learning.

We all have a lot of responsibility on our plates. We may be postponing coaching for a variety of reasons, with excuses such as:

Like planting trees, coaching takes time, pruning, and nurturing!

- *I will do it when others do it*, or
- *I will do it when there is a real need.*

This last reason suggests a crisis mentally. Coaching is like planting trees. It takes some time to grow them, and they require careful pruning and nurturing. In coaching, we must be able to plant, as well as harvest.

If we don't look long-term, we will strip-mine the relationship and create a heap of relationship overburden. One of our clients, who works in the agricultural business field, said it in farming terms, "Don't eat the seed corn." It means that if you don't stop and "sharpen the saw," you will put yourself into a vicious downward spiral.

Point Number 7

What return can you then expect from an investment in coaching and learning relationships? If the harvest is measured in loyalty, commitment, responsibility, openness, creativity, and talent, then both partners, as well as the organization, can benefit. Coaching is a solid foundation upon which to build. By placing trust in the coaching process, you can achieve constructive openness. Individuals, as well as the organizations to which they belong, will be able to move away from control, compliance, fear, confrontation, politics, and retaliation. If carefully applied, synergistic coaching allows an organization to build teams that are capable of achieving a new sense of achievement and personal worth, as well as a new and dynamic pulse. The result will be not only enhanced productivity, but organizations that move continually forward into the next century with focus and vision, and will become places where people want to be.

Point Number 8

If you appreciate at a deep level that "individuals" keep an organization fit, flexible, and vigorous, amazing things can be accomplished. You will need good partners to produce future learning and success. Likewise, these same individuals will help respond to the stormy times and downturns that any person or group will undoubtedly experience. If relationships remain healthy, and if effective communications develop, then positive influence will occur naturally. In addition, if the members of an organization help each other develop, learn, and improve—and thereby create synergy and creativity—then that organization will achieve impressive breakthroughs.

IN SUMMARY, coaching enables individuals to willingly contribute their energy and talent for the mutual benefit of the "whole."

It is our hope that you have gained some insights, and that we have also elicited a commitment to try them out. Gaining an appreciation for learning and coaching experiences is a positive, life-changing opportunity. Benjamin Franklin once stated that "Time is the stuff life is made of." If we could be so bold, perhaps we could conclude this book to you by saying that COACHING IS THE STUFF LEARNING AND LIFE ARE MADE OF!

Bibliographical References

Bibliographical References

Allen, James, *As A Man Thinketh.* Bookcraft, Salt Lake City.

Alicke, M.D., Braun, J.C., Glor, J.E., Klotz, M.L., Magee, J., Sederholm, H., and Siegel, R. Complaining behavior in social interactions. Personality and Social Psychology Bulletin, 18, 286-295, 1992.

Argyris, Chris, *Reasoning, Learning and Action: Individual and Organizational.* Josey Bass, San Francisco, Ca., 1982.

Cohen, Allan R, and Bradford, David L, *Influence Without Authority.* John Wiley and Sons, New York, 1989.

Conner, Daryl R, *Managing At The Speed Of Change.* Villard Books, New York, 1992. pp. 12.

Conner, *ODR Position Paper*, pp. 2.

Danziger, Sanford and Rivka, *You Are Your Own Best Counselor: The Life Pattern Handbook.* Self-mastery Systems International, Inc., Honolulu, 1984.

Didinger, Ray, *Game Plans For Success: Winning Strategies For Business And Life From 10 Top NFL Head Coaches*, NFL Properties Inc., 1995, pp. 81.

DePree, Max. *Leadership Is An Art.* Bantam Doubleday Dell Publishing Group, Inc., New York, 1989.

DePree, Max. *Leadership Jazz.* Bantam Doubleday Dell Publishing Group, Inc., New York, 1993.

Fisher, Roger, and Ury, William, *Getting To Yes: Negotiating Agreement Without Giving In.* Penguin Books, New York, 1991.

Frankl, Viktor, *Mans Search For Meaning.* Beacon Press, Boston, Ma., 1992.

Halper, Jan. *Quiet Desperation.* Warner Brooks, Inc., New York, 1988.

Kowalski, Robin M., *Complaints and Complaining: Functions, Antecedents, and Consequences.* Department of Psychology, Western Carolina University, Cullowhee, N.C., 1995.

Leary, M.R., and Shepperd, J.A. Behavioral Self-handicaps versus self-reported handicaps: A Conceptual Note. *Journal of Personality and Social Psychology,* 51, 1265-1268, 1986.

Mayer, Roger C., Davis, James H., and Schoorman, F. David, "An integrative Model Of Organizational Trust," *Academy of Management Review,* vol 20, no. 3, 1995, pp. 709-734.

McCullough, David, *Truman.* Simon & Schuster, New York, 1992 pp. 525, 857-858.

Phillips, Donald T., *Lincoln On Leadership.* Warner Books Inc., New York, 1992, pp. 173.

Senge, Peter. *The Fifth Discipline, The Art and Practice Of The Learning Organization.* Doubleday, New York, 1990, pp. 4.

Sims, Henry P., Jr., and Gioia, Dennis A. "Performance Failure: Executive Response to Self-Serving Bias." *Business Horizons.* January/February, 1984, pp. 64-71.

U.S. Department of Commerce, Bureau of The Census. *How We're Changing.* Special Studies. Series P23-191, February 1996.